THE VERSATILE RICE COOKER

Bob and Coleen Simmons

BRISTOL PUBLISHING ENTERPRISES, INC.
San Leandro, California

A Nitty Gritty® Cookbook

Printed in the United States of America.

ISBN 1-55867-068-8

Cover design: Frank Paredes
Cover photography: John Benson
Food stylist: Suzanne Carreiro
Illustrator: James Balkovek

CONTENTS

THE VERSATILE RICE COOKER

One half of the world's population eats rice at least once a day. For these people a rice cooker is the most sought-after kitchen appliance. Not only does it cook rice perfectly every time, but it will keep rice warm and delicious for several hours after cooking.

Because the cooker is always used for rice, usually cooked plain, other uses are rarely explored. The rice cooker makes a perfect vegetable steamer, and can be used to prepare a variety of delicious, healthful one-dish meals that can be served directly from the cooker. In addition we include several recipes that start with cooked rice for a base and some old favorite recipes that are served over cooked rice. Dim sum, the delightful Chinese snacks, can be easily made ahead and steamed in the rice cooker just before serving.

The rice cooker is a handy appliance for the home kitchen, the ski cabin, the dorm room or studio apartment. It is an all-purpose pot. Consider using it to cook frozen vegetables or entrées in pouches, or to steam fresh vegetables, fish or chicken. Cook pasta for two and then add the sauce to allow to heat through. It also can be used as a stew or soup pot, or for making risotto. By steaming foods to reheat you avoid drying them out as in the microwave oven.

The rice cooker is truly versatile, and here is a broad range of recipes and ideas that we think you will find interesting and delicious.

ABOUT RICE COOKERS

Rice cookers come in sizes from "3 cup" to those large enough to be suitable for a medium size Chinese restaurant. The size claimed by the manufacturer is the absolute maximum amount of uncooked rice that may be cooked in the cooker. If that amount of rice is cooked, it is possible that you will experience boil over and splashing.

All rice cookers work on the same principle. An inner pan sits on a heated plate which brings water in the pan to a boil. The water boils vigorously until it is absorbed by the food, or boils off as steam. A temperature sensor in contact with the pan feels the rise in temperature above that of boiling water and reduces the heat to "warm," which keeps the contents of the pan at the proper serving temperature without burning.

The primary cookers used to test the recipes in this book have 5- and 6-cup capacities. These cookers will cook as little as 1 cup of raw rice properly, and are large enough cook rice for a crowd or to steam enough vegetables for 3 or 4 persons.

RICE COOKER ACCESSORIES

The rice cooker usually comes with a small flat steamer rack or plate, a rice measuring cup and sometimes a round flat rice serving spoon. There are several other accessories that will make rice cooker cooking even easier. You may already have some of these items in your kitchen.

It is very desirable to have a collapsible stainless steel or plastic steamer basket. Buy one that fits easily into your cooker. Farberware makes a 9-inch black plastic one that works well. It has a detachable plastic handle that stays relatively cool when steaming.

A long-handled plastic spoon is very handy to have when using the rice cooker. Long-handled to keep your hands away from the steam and hot sides of the cooker when stirring or dishing up, and plastic so as not to scratch the finish in the bottom of the pan. This spoon is also handy for scraping the rice grains from the bottom of the pan during cleanup.

It is also convenient to have a platform to hold a steamer plate 2 to 3 inches above the pan bottom. We made a serviceable one by cutting the top and bottom from an 8-ounce can that had contained crushed pineapple. There also are inexpensive platforms, made expressly for the purpose, available where Chinese woks and accessories are sold.There is also an artichoke holder made of stainless steel that is perfect for holding a plate while steaming.

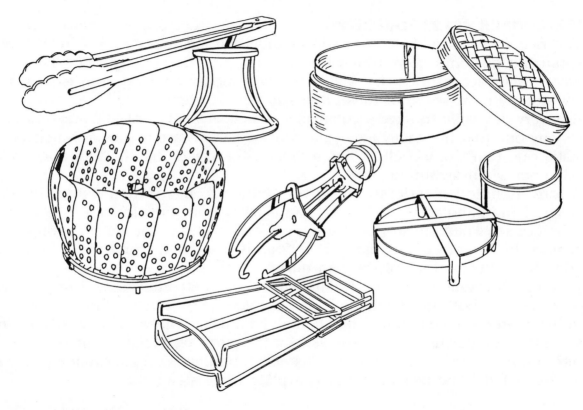

Depending on the size of your cooker pan, you may find a bamboo steamer basket that will fit down about half way into the cooker pan. The 8-inch size is perfect in a 5-cup cooker that is about 9 inches across the top.

Bamboo baskets can be stacked two or three high to steam individual plates of fish or chicken, and also make it possible to do larger quantities of dim sum or timbales. Use the bamboo lid on the top steamer. If necessary, wedge a clean dish towel between the steamer basket and the rice cooker pan to prevent loss of steam.

A plate lifter is very handy to help lift hot plates from the cooker or steamer baskets. Several varieties are available, and they are quite inexpensive.

HELPFUL HINTS

Always spray the rice cooker pan liberally with a good nonstick cooking spray such as PAM before cooking. If your pan is coated with Teflon or another special slick surface, spray it anyway. This will make cleanup much easier. The spray adds very little, either in cost or calories.

We use kosher salt in the rice cooker. It has no impurities or additives and dissolves easily. Salt measurements, when given in a recipe, are for table salt. When using kosher salt you need to use a little less than two times as much as you would if using common table salt.

Measuring cups that come with various brands of cookers differ in size. We assume that they are meant to be about the amount of rice for 1 portion. Please note that all our measurements are in standard cups.

When using the cooker as a steamer, if you allow the steamer to go dry and it shuts off, immediately unplug the cooker and pour ½ cup of cold water into the pan. This will ease cleanup.

The best way to clean the cooker pan is to fill it with warm soapy water and allow it to soak for a few minutes, and then use a plastic spoon or scrubber to loosen the adhering rice. Cooked rice does not come off in well in the dishwasher, and over time the dishwasher detergent will harm the hard annodized coating that is on most cooker pans.

Unlike most appliances, many rice cookers do not have an "on-off" switch, and must be unplugged to be totally off. Many have a pilot lamp to warn you that they are still on, but it is easy to forget to unplug the cooker after you have removed the food from it.

SAFETY CONSIDERATIONS

As with any appliance, there are things that one should keep constantly in mind.

1. When lifting the cover, always lift it away from your face and arms.

Steam can cause serious burns.

2. Don't allow the cooker cord to hang over the counter edge. A child can pull it off, or even brushing with an apron can pull a boiling pot off onto your feet and cause a serious burn.

3. Some rice cookers have an *on-off* switch, but most only have two states, *cook* and *warm*. After cooking, the appliance switches to *warm* and will keep cooked rice in perfect condition for serving for an hour or two. This is fine because plain cooked rice is not a good medium for bacterial growth. If, however, you cook other ingredients, especially chicken or seafood, with the rice, the contents of the cooker should be removed immediately after cooking to assure that no harmful bacteria multiply.

4. While not exactly a safety consideration, we discovered the hard way that it isn't wise to dispose of large quantities of cooked rice down the kitchen sink. This will eventually create a barrier that will defy drain cleaners. The best way to clean your cooker pan is to fill it with hot water and allow it to soak for a few minutes. Then scrape the grains that inevitably stick to the bottom of the pan with a plastic scraper or spoon. Pour the water through a strainer to catch the rice, and empty the strainer into the trash.

CHINESE RESTAURANT-STYLE RICE

The Chinese prefer rice that is not as sticky as Japanese rice but they still need a rice that is easily eaten with chopsticks. Chinese restaurants often cook a blend of rices, which is a mixture of long grain, medium grain and jasmine rices. The long grain is for texture, the jasmine provides fragrance, and the medium grain holds the cooked rice together so that it may be more easily eaten with chopsticks.

Chinese restaurants rarely salt steamed rice while it cooks. The rice serves as a foil for the savory, salty dishes that are served with it. A blend that works well for us is:

> ½ cup long grain rice
> ¼ cup jasmine rice
> ¼ cup medium grain rice

Add rice to cooker pan and wash well in three or four changes of water. Then drain well. Add 1¾ cup cooking water and salt if desired. Allow rice to soak for 15 minutes before turning on cooker. When cooker shuts off, fluff up the rice with a fork, replace cover, and steam for 10 minutes before serving.

INGREDIENTS

RICE

Most rice is eaten within a few miles of the paddy in which it grew, and in most places the locally grown rice is the only one available. We are very fortunate to have a variety of different rices from which to choose. Many dishes such as risotto and rice puddings are best when made with a specific type of rice. Here are some of the commonly available rices, and their characteristics.

LONG-GRAIN RICE

California - Cooks up soft and bland. Widely available. Hinode is a typical brand.

Carolina - No longer from the Carolinas, but grown in Texas and Louisiana. It is a little firmer and has more character than California rice. Mahatma is a commonly available brand.

Jasmine - From Thailand. Aromatic, but doesn't smell of flowers. The character is described as "earthy" or "nutty," neither of which is a perfect description. Has same appearance as long-grain. Cooks up soft and tender.

Texmati, Jasmati and California "basmati" - All are hybrids, with some characteristic Jasmine or basmati aroma.

Indian basmati - Grown in the Hymalayian foothills. True basmati has very long slender grains which stay separate when cooked. It is intensely fragrant and has a wonderful aroma while cooking. Basmati is the perfect accompaniment for curry, and makes wonderful pilafs. The finest basmati rices are aged for a year or two after harvest to enhance the aroma.

Parboiled - Widely available as *converted*. Specially processed to retain more vitamins and nutrients. Requires more water, and a longer cooking time than regular long-grain rice. Cooked grains are firm and stay separate.

MEDIUM-GRAIN RICE

Medium-grain rice is sold under a variety of names. The grains are about two times as long as they are round. Medium-grain rice is bland and slightly stickier than long grain. Medium-grain rice can be used in almost any recipe that calls for long grain.

SHORT-GRAIN RICE

Short-grain rice is also called *pearl* rice. Cooks up soft and sticky. This is the rice used to make sushi and rice pudding. Short-grain rice is not widely available, except in Asian and Puerto Rican markets.

Arborio rice - A very special short-grain rice imported from Italy. Used in risotto where it is cooked until just barely done in the center of the grain, and the surface starch creates a wonderful creamy sauce. It is possible to make delicious risotto in the rice cooker. Valencia rice from Spain which is generally used in paella is very similar to arborio, and the two can be used interchangeably.

BROWN RICE

During the milling process, brown rice has a portion or all of the bran layer left on the rice grains. Nutritionally, brown rice has more B-complex vitamins and much more fiber than polished rice. Almost any rice type can have the bran left on. The most popular brown rices are medium- and long-grain. Brown rice takes about three times as long to cook as polished rice, and the cooked rice retains a chewy texture. Since brown rice retains the germ and natural oils, it can turn stale and rancid if stored at room temperature for a long time. Buy only what you need for a month or two. Store in an airtight container in a cool dark place to preserve maximum freshness and flavor.

EXOTIC RICES AND BLENDS

Several rice producers market special hybrid rices and blends. One of our favorites is Konriko "Wild Pecan" rice. It is neither wild rice, nor does it contain pecans. It is hybrid rice specially processed to remove about 20% of the bran which allows it to cook in just slightly more time than polished rice. The flavor is nutty and delicious. Lundberg Farms markets several distinctive blends of rice. We especially like their Wild Blend, which is a combination of brown, sweet Wehani and black Japonica varieties. There are many other specialty rices available, as well as spiced and flavored rice. All cook well in the rice cooker. Follow package cooking instructions.

RICE STORAGE AND COOKING

White rice will keep indefinitely if stored in an airtight container in a dark, cool place. Brown rice has a limited storage life, so buy only a two or three months supply. Some people like very soft rice while others prefer individual grains with some resistance to the bite. The softness of rice cooked in the cooker can be controlled by the amount of water added. Start out following package directions, and adjust the water to your taste. When the amount of rice is doubled, it isn't necessary to double the water. About ⅔ more is usually adequate. Salt the cooking water if desired. About ½ teaspoon of salt for each cup of uncooked rice is a good starting place. If the rice is to be served plain, a tablespoon of butter or margarine added to the cooking water for each cup will give the rice a nice silky texture and will keep the grains more separate. When the cooker shuts off, fluff up the rice with a fork and immediately replace the cooker cover. Allow to steam for 10 minutes more for perfect rice.

THE RICE COOKER PANTRY

Cooking in the rice cooker is fast and if you have some of these basic pantry items, you can quickly put together a satisfying dinner.

Nonstick cooking spray - There are many nonstick cooking sprays on the market. Names with wide market recognition are marketed as Pam, Mazola and Bertolli. There are vegetable and olive oil sprays available, and both do an excellent job, adding few calories. Spraying the rice cooker container with these sprays makes clean-up a much easier task, particularly since you don't want to use an abrasive scrubber on the special finishes of the rice cooking pan.

Olive oils - There is a wide range of olive oils available from Italy, Spain, France, Greece and California. They run the gambit in color from pale yellow to deep green, and from light and elegant to robust and full-flavored. Most of the rice salads and many other recipes in this book call for full-flavored olive oil because it adds another layer of aroma and taste. In order to appreciate the difference in various oils, buy the smallest bottles of several different kinds and have a tasting. Pour a small amount of each in a little saucer, look at the color, smell it, dip a small cube of fresh crusty bread into each and taste each one. Then buy more of the one that has the best flavor and aroma for your taste. You will want to have at least one extra virgin olive oil and one or two full-flavored virgin or pure olive oils on hand. Extra virgin oils are hand-pressed oils and generally are not used for frying because they lose fragrance and charm when heated, and tend to burn more easily.

Olive oils have a limited shelf life after opening, so buy only the amount that you will use in a reasonable time. Olive oil should be stored in a dark, cool place, but not in the refrigerator.

Bouillon cubes - Of the many different bouillon cubes in the market we have found Knorr to be our favorite. Bouillon cubes are available in chicken, beef, fish and vegetable flavors. If you don't have broth or stock on hand, add a regular sized cube for each cup of liquid, or a large cube for each pint to any of the recipes in this book to add a little extra flavor to the dish. Most bouillon cubes are quite salty, so remember to reduce the salt when using them.

Canned tomato pieces - There is a short period of a couple of months in the summer when tomatoes are at their very tastiest. By all means, use ripe fresh tomatoes if you have them. For the rest of the year, and for recipes that call for long cooking, substitute canned tomatoes. These are processed at their peak of perfection and outshine the tasteless, hard product found in the market after prime season. Italian-style canned tomatoes, usually Romanos, are fleshy plum shaped tomatoes with few seeds. These should be prepared by cutting out the hard stems, and squeezing out the seeds, using a strainer to catch the seeds and pass through the juice. Discard the seeds, chop the tomatoes and add them with their juice to the dish. One of the handiest tomato products on the market is canned ready-cut tomato pieces which are diced and packed in juice. The ratio of tomato to juice is very high and we recommend using them for most of these recipes because they are a very good substitute for fresh tomatoes without peeling, seeding and dicing.

Canned chicken and beef broth - Canned chicken and beef stocks not labeled as low sodium tend to be quite salty. We have found the "broths" to be much lighter and less concentrated. Rice cooker cooking with its intense boiling tends to concentrate flavors and saltiness. If you use salted stock or broth, reduce the amount of salt added or you may end up with a saltier dish than you anticipated.

Dehydrated and freeze-dried vegetables - In these busy days when it is important to save time and still prepare nutritious foods for quick dinners, the dehydrated and freeze-dried vegetables available on the spice shelves of your supermarket can be tremendous time savers. They are very high quality, and it is difficult to tell the difference from fresh after they have been boiled for a few minutes in liquid. If you prefer, and have fresh vegetables on hand, however, do substitute them for dried after you have sautéed them in a little oil, butter or wine to soften before adding to the rice cooker.

Onions. Peeling and cutting up onions isn't anyone's favorite job. Because most of the rice preparations cook for at least 15 minutes, dehydrated onion can be used when onion is called for in the recipe. Nationally known manufacturers, such as Schilling and Spice Islands, produce dehydrated onion flakes, and it is an excellent product.

Celery flakes. How many times have you purchased a bunch of celery and used 2 to 3 stalks, storing the rest in the vegetable drawer until it is over the hill? A teaspoon or tablespoon of dried celery flakes adds celery flavor without the necessity of browning in fat to soften it for a recipe.

Peppers. Green and red bell pepper pieces, sweet red pepper flakes and spicy dried pepper flakes are all available on the spice shelves of your supermarket. If fresh peppers aren't available, or you don't want to take the time to peel and dice them, these products also soften and add flavor to many recipes done in the rice cooker.

Chives. Freeze-dried chives are one of the better freeze-dried vegetables. Fresh chives are becoming more available year-round in the market, but the dried product has great texture and taste. Substitute them for fresh in almost any dish.

Garlic. Freeze-dried garlic is amazingly pungent and garlic-flavored. Use for those recipes when requested.

Parsley. Dried parsley has a weedy aroma when you smell it. It doubles nicely for fresh when you don't feel like washing and mincing the fresh. It takes only seconds to reconstitute in a little liquid.

Mushrooms. Freeze-dried mushroom slices or pieces give dishes a real mushroom flavor. They cook quickly and can be added straight from the jar to any dish that boils for a few minutes. Dried mushrooms include the intensely flavored Italian porcini and the Asian shiitake. Both must be soaked before adding to a dish. Use the strained soaking water in the recipe for a more intense flavor.

QUICK AND EASY RICE RECIPES

Everyone needs some fast, delicious dishes that can be done with a minimum of chopping and cooking. Here is a collection of savory recipes that are done completely in the rice cooker, from rice cooked with spices or flavored broths, to vegetables or seafood added the last 10 minutes while the rice steams. Also included are a *Seafood Risotto* and a *Red Pepper and Mushroom Risotto* which are cooked in the classic manner in an uncovered rice cooker. There is also an easy, no-stir version for the nights you don't want to fuss. Consider cooking some of the different frozen vegetables or soup mixes with rice to make new quick and easy favorites.

SAN ANTONIO RICE

Stir a carton of your favorite fresh salsa into the rice cooker, add rice and some fresh corn kernels, and you have a flavorful supper or side dish for grilled chicken or fish.

1 cup uncooked long-grain rice
1 carton (12 oz.) fresh salsa, mild or hot
1 tbs. vegetable oil
1 can (11 oz.) Mexicorn with juice
½ tsp. cumin
½ tsp. salt, freshly ground pepper
1¼ cups water
fresh cilantro for garnish

Spray rice cooker container with nonstick cooking spray. Add all ingredients except cilantro, stir, cover and cook. When liquid has evaporated, lift cover, quickly stir and replace cover. Allow to steam for 8 to 10 minutes before serving. Spoon into a warm serving dish, garnish with fresh cilantro and serve.

THAI-STYLE RICE

Servings: 3 to 4

Make this rice to serve with spicy foods. The coconut milk adds flavor and richness.

1 cup long-grain Jasmine rice
2 cups canned coconut milk
¼ tsp. ground cardamom
½ tsp. ground coriander
¼ tsp. salt
slivered fresh basil leaves or cilantro leaves for garnish

Spray rice cooker container with nonstick cooking spray. Add all ingredients except for basil or cilantro. Cover and cook until rice cooker shuts off, about 20 minutes. Allow to stand 10 minutes before serving.

LEMON DILL RICE

Servings: 4

This lemony rice is great with fish and chicken dishes. The lemon and herbs cook with the rice.

1 cup long-grain Jasmine rice
1¾ cups water
½ tsp. salt
grated rind from one lemon
1 tbs. lemon juice
½ tsp. dried dill weed
1 tbs. fresh parsley, minced, or 1 tsp. dried
2 tbs. butter, cut into 4 pieces

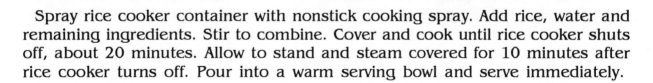

Spray rice cooker container with nonstick cooking spray. Add rice, water and remaining ingredients. Stir to combine. Cover and cook until rice cooker shuts off, about 20 minutes. Allow to stand and steam covered for 10 minutes after rice cooker turns off. Pour into a warm serving bowl and serve immediately.

EASY RISOTTO

This no-stir version of risotto uses dried mushrooms and spices, and makes a delicious creamy first course or side dish.

4 tbs. butter
3/4 cup white onion, minced
1 cup Silver Pearl medium-grain rice
2 cans (14.5 oz. each) chicken broth
1/2 cup freeze-dried mushroom pieces

2 tbs. dried parsley
1/4 tsp. dried sage
1/3 cup dry white or red wine
pinch of white pepper
1/2 cup grated Parmesan cheese

Spray rice cooker container with nonstick spray and set it to cook. Add butter to container. When butter has melted, sauté onion for 3 to 4 minutes until softened. Add rice and continue to cook for 2 to 3 minutes, coating rice with butter. Add chicken broth and all remaining ingredients except Parmesan cheese. Cover and cook until rice cooker shuts off. Remove cover, stir in Parmesan cheese, and serve immediately on warm plates or in a warm bowl.

ORANGE RICE PILAF

This is a delicious accompaniment for almost any fish, chicken or pork dish.

2 tbs. butter
¼ cup onion, finely chopped, or 1 tbs. dried onion flakes
grated rind of 1 orange
juice of 2 oranges plus enough chicken stock to make 1¾ cups liquid
1 cup long-grain rice
½ tsp. salt
¼ cup slivered toasted almonds for garnish

Spray rice cooker container with nonstick cooking spray. Add all ingredients except toasted almonds. Cover and cook until liquid evaporates, about 20 minutes. Allow to stand for 10 minutes. Spoon into a warm serving bowl, top with toasted almonds and serve immediately.

RISI E BISI

This traditional Italian dish is a tasty accompaniment to roast chicken and grilled fish, or double the recipe for serving as part of a buffet. For the buffet table, spoon the cooked rice into radicchio cups or hollowed-out tomatoes and place on a platter.

2 tbs. butter
1½ cups chicken stock
1 cup long-grain rice
¼ cup dry white wine
2 tbs. freeze-dried onion flakes
½ tsp. thyme
salt and white pepper

1½ cups frozen peas, rinsed with
   cold water
¼ cup diced smoked ham or
   prosciutto, optional
1 tsp. minced chives, fresh or
   freeze-dried
grated Parmesan cheese, optional

Spray rice cooker container with nonstick cooking spray. Place butter in container and turn to cook. Allow butter to melt and then add all ingredients except peas, ham and chives. Cover and allow to cook until rice cooker shuts off. Carefully lift the cover, stir rice and add peas, diced ham and chives. Cover and allow to steam for 10 minutes. Serve with grated Parmesan cheese, if desired.

QUICK MUSHROOM HERB RICE

Servings: 4

The freeze-dried mushrooms and vegetables are delicious in this rice preparation. "Wild Pecan" rice has more pecan aroma than taste, and is a great Southern product.

2⅓ cups water
1 box (7 oz.) "Wild Pecan" rice
2 tbs. butter
⅓ cup freeze-dried mushroom pieces
1 tbs. freeze-dried green pepper
1 tbs. freeze-dried celery flakes
1 tbs. dehydrated onion
1 pinch each black and white pepper
1 tsp. salt
several drops of red pepper sauce

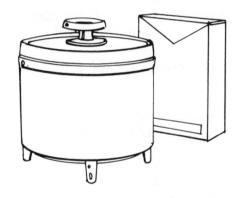

Spray rice cooker container with nonstick spray. Pour in water and add remaining ingredients; stir gently to combine. Cover and cook until rice cooker clicks off. Carefully remove lid, stir and replace cover. Allow to steam for 15 minutes before serving. Stir well and spoon into a warm serving dish.

SEAFOOD RISOTTO

Servings: 2 to 3

This is a classic seafood risotto. It is important to use Arborio or other short-grain rice, and keep the chicken stock very hot while you add it to the rice. Typically, risottos are more moist than regular cooked rice, and you only add liquid to the point the rice is still firm but does not have a hard center when you bite into it. This recipe can be easily doubled and makes a delicious appetizer or dinner entrée.

2½ to 2¾ cups chicken stock
1 tbs. butter
1 tbs. light olive oil
½ cup onion, finely chopped
1 garlic clove, minced
1 cup Arborio or other short-grain
  rice
½ cup white wine
1 tbs. lemon juice

½ tsp. dried tarragon
1 tbs. dried parsley, or 2 tbs. fresh
  minced
dash hot pepper flakes
¼ lb. small shrimp, peeled and
  deveined
¼ lb. scallops, washed and small
  side muscle removed
salt and freshly ground pepper

Bring chicken stock to a boil in the microwave or on the stovetop. Spray rice cooker container with nonstick spray. Turn rice cooker on to cook and melt butter and oil. Add onion and garlic, cook 1 to 2 minutes and then add rice. Stir to coat rice with butter mixture. Add white wine, lemon juice, dried tarragon, parsley and hot pepper flakes. Slowly add hot chicken stock about 1/3 cup at a time to rice, stirring constantly, waiting until rice absorbs most of the liquid before adding more stock. In about 15 to 18 minutes taste a rice grain to see if it is tender. Drain shrimp and scallops on paper towels, pat dry, and add to rice with salt and pepper. Continue to cook, stirring 1 to 2 minutes just until seafood is cooked. Pour into a warm serving bowl and serve immediately.

RED PEPPER AND MUSHROOM RISOTTO   Servings: 4

Almost any vegetable is wonderful cooked in a risotto. Replace red pepper with peas and snow pea pods, or coarsely grated carrots and slivered leeks. Bring the chicken stock to a boil and keep it very hot while you are adding it to the rice.

3 tbs. olive oil
½ cup chopped onion
1 cup coarsely chopped mushrooms
½ cup diced red pepper, peeled and
  seeded
1 cup Arborio or short-grain rice

3 to 3¼ cups chicken stock
1 tbs. dried parsley
½ cup diced ham or Canadian bacon
dash red pepper flakes
salt and freshly ground pepper
½ cup grated Parmesan cheese

Bring chicken stock to a boil in the microwave or on the stovetop. Spray rice cooker container with nonstick spray. Turn rice cooker on to cook and heat oil. Add onion and cook 3 to 4 minutes until onion softens. Add mushrooms and red pepper. Continue to cook 3 to 4 minutes. Stir in rice and cook for 2 minutes until rice is well coated. Add parsley, ham, red pepper flakes, salt and pepper. Slowly add hot chicken stock about ⅓ cup at a time to rice, stirring constantly, waiting until rice absorbs most of the liquid before adding more stock. In about 15 to 18 minutes taste a rice grain to see if it is tender. Spoon into a warm serving bowl, toss with Parmesan cheese and serve immediately.

TUNA AND SPINACH RICE

Everyone has a favorite tuna and rice dish. This version uses frozen creamed spinach and some lemon zest for a new look. Sprinkle with finely grated cheddar cheese just before serving if you like that combination.

1 cup uncooked long-grain rice
2 cups water
1 tbs. dehydrated onion flakes
½ tsp. salt
freshly ground black pepper
1 can (6½ oz.) tuna packed in oil, drained, oil reserved
1 tsp. grated lemon zest
1 pkg. (10 oz.) creamed spinach, defrosted
cheddar cheese, optional

Spray rice cooker container with nonstick cooking spray. Add rice, water, onion, salt, pepper and oil from tuna. Cover and cook until rice cooker shuts off. Carefully remove cover and stir in tuna, lemon zest, and creamed spinach. Cover and allow to steam 10 minutes before serving. Top with grated cheddar cheese, if desired.

TRADITIONAL RICE FAVORITES

There are some dishes that are automatically thought of when rice is mentioned. These are either served over rice or rice is an important component, such as *Chicken Cacciatore, Beef Stroganoff* and *Chili*. Chinese-style fried rice made with leftover cold cooked rice is wonderful served for breakfast, lunch or dinner. Curry demands a great mound of hot cooked rice and our *Easy Curry Sauce* can be made ahead right in the rice cooker. The rice cooker also works well for cooking small rice and grape leaf *Dolma* packages.

QUICK FRIED RICE

This recipe alone is reason enough for cooking more rice than you need for dinner. Cold cooked rice is a must for good fried rice. Rub rice clumps between your fingers to break them into individual grains. For variation use leftover cooked asparagus or broccoli instead of peas.

3 tbs. vegetable oil
4 green onions, thinly sliced
3 cups cold cooked rice, crumbled
2 eggs, lightly beaten
½ cup diced cooked ham, chicken, sausage or shrimp

½ cup frozen green peas, rinsed with cold water
2 tbs. soy sauce
1 tsp. sesame oil
⅛ tsp. white pepper
fresh cilantro leaves for garnish

Heat vegetable oil in a wok or large nonstick skillet. Sauté onions 1 to 2 minutes to soften. Add crumbled rice and cook 3 to 4 minutes over medium heat, stirring constantly. Make a well in middle of rice and pour in beaten eggs. When eggs start to set, stir into rice. Add ham, green peas, soy sauce and sesame oil. Season with pepper and continue to cook for 1 minute until mixture is hot. Garnish with cilantro and serve in a warm bowl or on warm plates.

DOLMAS

These are wonderful for party appetizers, lunches or picnic fare, and keep well for several days in the refrigerator. Use leftover grape leaves to wrap around salmon or chicken before steaming or grilling.

3 tbs. full-flavored olive oil
½ finely chopped onion
1 clove garlic, minced
salt and freshly ground pepper
½ lb. mushrooms, chopped
2 tbs. lemon juice
¾ cup cooked long-grain rice

½ tsp. dill weed
2 tbs. minced parsley
2 tbs. pine nuts or chopped almonds
1 jar (8 oz.) grape leaves in brine
¼ cup lemon juice
2 tbs. full-flavored olive oil
3 cups water

Heat 3 tbs. olive oil in a medium nonstick skillet and sauté onion 3 to 4 minutes until translucent. Raise heat, add garlic, salt, pepper, chopped mushrooms and lemon juice. Cook for 3 to 4 minutes until mushrooms are tender. Stir in cooked rice, dill weed, parsley and pine nuts.

Rinse grape leaves in cold water. Separate, trim long stems with scissors and pat dry with paper towels. Place leaves shiny side down on a plate or board. To fill, place 1 tbs. of rice mixture near the stem end and roll up jelly roll fashion, tucking in sides of leaves to make a neat package as you roll. If leaves are extra large, trim a little from sides so the wrapper doesn't overwhelm the filling. If there is a tear in the leaf, patch with a piece of trimmed excess or a piece from another leaf.

Spray rice cooker container and steamer plate with nonstick spray. Place dolmas in one layer on the steamer plate. Add ¼ cup lemon juice, 2 tbs. olive oil and 3 cups water. Liquid should come part way up sides of dolmas. Place a plate on top of dolmas, leaving a small space between plate and sides of cooker for steam to circulate. Cover rice cooker and cook for 20 minutes. Turn off and remove cover. Allow to stand until plate is cool enough to lift out. Place warm dolmas on a plate. Serve warm at room temperature, or cover and refrigerate until ready to serve.

Note: If using smaller than an 8-cup rice cooker, cook dolmas in two batches.

HOPPIN' JOHN

Servings: 4 to 6

This is a traditional Southern dish eaten on New Year's Day to bring good luck. Blackeyed peas and rice are cooked together with either bacon or ham and typically served with cornbread and a side dish of greens.

2 cans (15 oz.) blackeyed peas with juice
water
1 cup medium-grain rice
1½ cups diced smoked ham
2 tbs. dried onion flakes

2 garlic cloves, minced
2 tbs. dried parsley
¼ tsp. dried thyme
generous dash red pepper flakes
2 tbs. lemon juice
freshly ground pepper

Spray rice cooker container with nonstick spray. Drain pea liquid into a measuring cup and add enough water to make 2½ cups. Add liquid and remaining ingredients except canned blackeyed peas to rice cooker. Cover and cook until rice cooker shuts off. Carefully remove cover, add canned peas and quickly stir peas into rice. Recover and allow to steam for 10 minutes before serving.

CHILI

This is another hearty favorite to serve over freshly cooked hot rice.

1½ lb. ground chuck
1 large yellow onion, chopped
4 garlic cloves, minced
¼ cup prepared chili powder
1 can (28 oz.) ready-cut tomatoes with juice
1 tbs. Worcestershire sauce
2 cups beef broth
salt and freshly ground pepper to taste

Brown ground meat in a large skillet, crumbling it into small pieces as it cooks. Pour meat and fat into a strainer over a bowl to drain. Add back about 2 tbs. fat to skillet and cook onion and garlic over low heat 4 to 5 minutes to soften onion. Add meat and remaining ingredients to skillet. Simmer uncovered for about 30 minutes. Serve in bowls over hot rice.

EASY CURRY SAUCE

This moderately spicy curry sauce can be easily made in less than 30 minutes and freezes beautifully. Make the sauce ahead, and then add cooked meat or chicken to the hot sauce and cook 10 minutes to combine flavors just before serving. Raw shrimp or fish should be added to the hot sauce and cooked only 3 to 4 minutes, just until done. A fresh fruit salad or **Cucumber Raita,** *page 65, makes a cooling accompaniment.*

3 tbs. butter
2 to 3 tsp. curry powder, depending on hotness desired
3 cups chicken stock
1 small green apple, peeled, cored, chopped
2 tbs. dried onion
1 tbs. freeze-dried mixed vegetables
1 tbs. freeze-dried sweet pepper flakes
1 tbs. freeze-dried celery flakes
1 tsp. dried dill weed
1 tsp. dried cumin
dash hot pepper flakes

½ tsp. salt
1 slice fresh ginger
1½ to 2 cups diced cooked chicken or meat or uncooked seafood
hot cooked rice
condiments: chopped peanuts, shredded unsweetened coconut, chutney,
  raisins or dried cherries

Spray rice cooker container with nonstick spray. Place butter in bottom of rice cooker container, turn cooker on and allow butter to melt. Stir in curry powder and cook 1 to 2 minutes to bring out curry flavors. Add chicken stock, apple, vegetables, spices and fresh ginger. Bring to a boil; cook uncovered for 20 minutes, stirring occasionally to prevent sticking. If serving immediately, add meat or fish of your choice and heat through.

Serve over hot rice with your choice of condiments. Makes 2¼ cups.

CHICKEN GUMBO

Servings: 6

This flavorful stew is served in shallow bowls over cooked rice. It can be made ahead and refrigerated for 1 to 2 days before serving. The skinless, boneless chicken thighs now available in freezer packs make this a quick dish to put together.

3 tbs. butter
3 tbs. flour
3 slices bacon, cut in ½-inch pieces
6 boneless, skinless chicken thighs
1 tbs. dried celery flakes
2 large onions, chopped
1 green pepper, chopped
1 can (14 oz.) tomato pieces with
  juice
½ tsp. thyme
¼ tsp. white pepper

¼ tsp. (or more) Tabasco
3 cups chicken stock
1 pkg. (10 oz.) frozen sliced okra,
  defrosted
6 oz. Polish or Andouille sausage,
  sliced ¼-inch thick
½ cup diced smokey ham, optional
salt and pepper
6 to 8 cups hot cooked long-grain
  rice

Make a roux in a small frying pan by cooking butter and flour together over low heat until the color of peanut butter. Set aside. Cut chicken thighs into 6 to 7 pieces each. Fry bacon pieces in a large heavy saucepan or deep skillet. Remove bacon and pour out all but 2 tablespoons of bacon fat.

Sauté celery, onions and pepper in bacon fat for 5 to 6 minutes until soft. Add chicken and cook for 3 to 4 minutes, stirring constantly. Add tomatoes, thyme, white pepper, Tabasco, chicken stock and roux. Bring mixture to a boil and add okra, sausages, ham, salt and pepper. Simmer covered for 30 minutes, stirring occasionally. Place hot cooked rice in bowls and ladle gumbo over rice. Pass the Tabasco sauce for those who like it really spicy.

CHICKEN CACCIATORE

Servings: 3 to 4

Serve this flavorful chicken with mushroom and tomato sauce over mounds of freshly cooked hot rice. This dish can be made ahead and refrigerated for serving the next day.

6 chicken thighs, skinned
salt, pepper, flour
3 tbs. full-flavored olive oil
½ lb. mushrooms, sliced
½ cup chopped onion
2 garlic cloves, minced
3 tomatoes, peeled, seeded, chopped
¼ cup white wine or dry sherry
2 tbs. brandy
1 tbs. Worcestershire sauce
½ tsp. each tarragon, thyme, oregano
1 tbs. dried parsley flakes, or ¼ cup fresh
½ tsp. grated lemon rind
salt and freshly ground pepper

Lightly coat chicken with salt, pepper and flour and sauté in olive oil in a large skillet. When chicken is lightly browned on each side, remove to a plate. Add mushrooms and cook 3 to 4 minutes until they soften. Add onion and garlic; cook 2 to 3 minutes. Add chicken pieces and remaining ingredients. Bring liquid to a boil, cover and cook over low heat for 30 minutes. Turn chicken pieces once or twice during cooking. If sauce appears thin, remove cover and cook over high heat 5 to 10 minutes to reduce sauce. Serve immediately over hot rice. Cool slightly and refrigerate if not eating right away.

BEEF STROGANOFF

This is a classic favorite to be served over hot cooked rice. Make the meat sauce ahead and add the sour cream just before reheating and serving. This also freezes well without the mushrooms and sour cream.

1 lb. flank steak, cut into ½-inch by 2-inch strips
2 tbs. butter
½ cup chopped onion
1 garlic clove, minced
1 large tomato, peeled, seeded, chopped or ½ cup canned tomato pieces, drained
1 tbs. Worcestershire sauce
6 to 8 drops Tabasco
½ cup beef or chicken stock
salt and freshly ground pepper
2 tbs. butter
½ lb. mushrooms, sliced
1 cup sour cream

Lightly brown steak pieces in butter 3 to 4 minutes. Add onion, garlic, tomato pieces, Worcestershire sauce, Tabasco, beef stock, salt and pepper. Cook covered over low heat for 20 minutes. In another skillet, heat butter and brown mushrooms. Just before serving, combine mushrooms and sour cream with meat mixture and heat through but do not boil. Serve immediately on hot cooked rice.

JAMBALAYA

This dish has many variations and can be made with leftover cooked chicken or ham. A few shrimp tossed in during the last few minutes of steaming are good, too.

2 tbs. full-flavored olive oil
1 cup onion, coarsely chopped
1 red pepper, peeled and diced
1 cup uncooked long-grain rice
1 tsp. dried celery flakes
1¾ cups chicken broth
1 can (14 oz.) tomato pieces with juice
1 tbs. tomato paste

½ tsp. thyme
½ tsp. salt and freshly ground pepper
dash powdered cloves
¼ tsp. chili powder
1 tbs. dried parsley flakes
6 to 8 drops Tabasco
⅓ cup diced ham
6 oz. Polish sausage (about 1¼ cups), cut into slices

Spray rice cooker container with nonstick cooking spray. Turn rice cooker on and place oil in cooking container. When it begins to get hot, sauté onion and red pepper for 3 to 4 minutes to soften. Add rice and stir to coat. Add remaining ingredients, cover and cook, stirring once or twice, until rice cooker turns off. Allow jambalaya to steam for about 10 minutes before serving.

WILD RICE

Wild rice isn't really a rice at all, but a grass that grows in the U.S. and Canada in an area surrounding the upper Great Lakes. Wild rice has a delicious nutty flavor and chewy texture. Formerly wild rice was very expensive, but it has become more reasonably priced with the cultivation of large fields in California.

PLAIN WILD RICE

Wild rice adds an interesting texture and distinctive taste when served as a side dish or combined with other ingredients.

1 cup wild rice, rinsed under cold water
3½ cups chicken stock or water
½ tsp. salt

Spray rice cooker container with nonstick spray. Place rice, chicken stock or water and salt in rice cooker. Cover and cook until rice cooker shuts off, about 40 minutes. Allow rice to steam 10 minutes. The grains will be whole and chewy. If you prefer a softer wild rice add more water. As the rice cooks longer, the grains tend to split open and become softer. Serve hot rice as an accompaniment to roast meats or chicken. Or use in *Wild Rice and Raisin Timbales*, page 48.

WILD RICE AND SAUSAGE

Servings: 4

Sausages are a natural flavor combination with wild rice, adding spice and texture. Serve this as a main dish accompanied by cranberry sauce or applesauce, or use it to stuff Cornish game hens.

2 Italian sausages, mild or hot
1 cup uncooked wild rice
3½ cups beef broth
1 tbs. dehydrated onion
1 tsp. dried garlic
2 tbs. freeze-dried parsley
¼ cup freeze-dried mushroom pieces, optional
freshly ground pepper

Remove sausage casings and sauté sausage in a small skillet until lightly browned, crumbling it into small pieces as it cooks. Spray rice cooker container with nonstick cooking spray. Put in remaining ingredients and cooked sausage with its fat. Cover and cook until rice cooker shuts off. Allow to steam for 10 minutes before serving.

WILD RICE AND RAISIN TIMBALES   Makes 4 to 6 timbales

These savory molds are a delicious accompaniment for the holiday roast turkey or ham, or serve with roast chicken or pork. Substitute chopped dried apricots for the raisins for another interesting variation.

2 tbs. butter
1/2 cup onion, chopped
1 1/2 cups cooked wild rice
1/2 cup white raisins
2 eggs
1/4 cup heavy cream
1 tsp. Worcestershire sauce
1/4 tsp. thyme
1 tbs. dried parsley, or 2 tbs. chopped fresh
salt and freshly ground black pepper

Melt butter in a small nonstick skillet. Sauté onions 5 to 6 minutes until soft. In a medium bowl, beat eggs and cream; add Worcestershire, thyme, parsley, salt and pepper. Fold in wild rice, raisins and cooked onions.

Spray four 5- to 6-oz. custard cups or six 4-oz. timbales with nonstick spray. Fill molds about ¾ full of rice mixture. Cover each mold with foil, crimping foil securely at top of mold. Spray rice cooker container and steamer plate with nonstick spray. Add about 2½ cups water to rice cooker; place molds on steamer plate. Cover rice cooker and turn it on. Steam 5- to 6-oz. molds about 20 minutes after water boils; small molds should be steamed about 15 to 18 minutes.

Remove molds from cooker with kitchen tongs. Allow to stand about 5 minutes before uncovering and unmolding. To unmold, run a sharp knife blade around edge of timbale, place a plate upside down on top of timbale and invert. The timbale will unmold easily.

WILD RICE FRITTATA

Servings: 2 to 3

Wild rice adds an interesting flavor and texture to the Italian-style egg frittata. This is great lunch box or picnic fare.

2 small dried black Shiitaki mushrooms
3 tbs. full-flavored olive oil
5 to 6 green onions, thinly sliced
4 eggs
1 cup cooked wild rice
2 fresh tomatoes, peeled, seeded, chopped
2 tbs. Parmesan cheese
1/4 tsp. dried tarragon
1 tsp. Worcestershire sauce
salt and freshly ground pepper
grated Parmesan cheese for topping

Preheat oven to 400°. Cover dried mushrooms with boiling water and allow to stand for 15 minutes to soften. Remove from water, squeeze very dry, and cut out tough stem. Cut into small thin slivers.

Heat 2 tbs. olive oil in a 7- to 8-inch ovenproof skillet. Sauté onions and mushroom slivers 2 to 3 minutes. In a medium bowl, lightly beat eggs with a fork. Add onions, mushrooms and remaining ingredients to egg mixture except for Parmesan cheese. Spray skillet with nonstick spray and add remaining tablespoon of olive oil.

When oil is hot, swirl it around sides of skillet, and pour in egg mixture. Cook until eggs start to set, lifting up mixture at sides of pan so uncooked portion flows under cooked egg. When most of mixture has set, sprinkle with Parmesan cheese and place in preheated oven. Bake about 10 minutes until the mixture is firm to the touch and lightly browned. Remove from oven and slide out of pan onto a plate lined with paper towels to drain. Slide onto a warm serving plate and cut into wedges. Serve warm or at room temperature.

WILD RICE PANCAKES

Serve these for breakfast with a maple or fruit syrup, or top with creamed chicken or turkey to make a substantial lunch or brunch dish.

3 eggs, separated
¾ cup milk
2 tbs. melted butter
⅓ cup flour
½ tsp. salt
¾ cup cooked wild rice

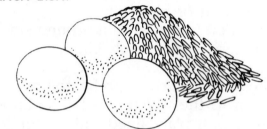

Preheat griddle. Separate eggs. Place egg yolks in a medium bowl and beat until well combined. Stir in milk, butter, flour and salt. Add wild rice. In a separate bowl, beat egg whites until stiff but not dry. Gently fold egg whites into rice mixture. Cook pancakes on lightly oiled griddle. Serve immediately.

SALADS

Rice salads are always popular and for good reason. Rice is a wonderful foil for zesty black olives, capers, anchovies and full-flavored olive oils and aromatic vinegars. A few chopped crisp vegetables add color and texture. Rice also is easily pressed into ring molds, or a small bowl, or spread on a platter to make a beautiful presentation. *Party Rice Ring* and *Rice Salad Niçoise* are two of the prettiest, and most delicious, in this section.

Fresh rice cooker-steamed vegetables also make wonderful salads. Warm new potatoes are dressed with a simple vinaigrette, or combined with smoked salmon for a more sophisticated treat.

Rice salads tend to be a little dry in texture if they are refrigerated for many hours. They are best made and served the same day; however, they can be refrigerated and a little extra dressing added just before serving.

TURKEY SAUSAGE BROWN RICE SALAD

Servings: 4

Use low fat smoked turkey sausage in this flavorful salad. Make the salad as soon as rice and sausage have cooled. This salad keeps for 2 to 3 days in the refrigerator.

1 cup uncooked long-grain brown rice
2¼ cups water
1 tsp. dried onion flakes, optional
½ cup low fat smoked turkey sausage, diced
⅓ cup carrot, coarsely grated
2 tbs. red onion, finely chopped

3 tbs. celery, finely chopped
3 tbs. sweet pickle, diced
2 tbs. parsley, minced
1 tbs. Dijon mustard
2 tbs. full-flavored olive oil
1 tbs. cider vinegar
salt and freshly ground pepper

Spray rice cooker container with nonstick spray. Add rice, water, onion flakes and smoked sausage. Cover and cook until liquid has evaporated, about 50 minutes. Check rice when steamer goes off to see if grains are tender. If still a little crunchy, recover and continue to steam for another 10 to 15 minutes. Pour rice out on a shallow plate and allow to cool a few minutes. When rice is barely warm, add remaining ingredients and mix well. Cover and refrigerate for 1 to 2 hours before serving so the flavors can combine.

PARTY RICE RING

This colorful salad is formed in a ring mold. Fill the center with a creamy chicken salad, colorful cherry tomatoes or a hot green vegetable.

1 cup long-grain rice
1 chicken bouillon cube
2 cups water
2 tbs. full-flavored olive oil
2 tbs. sherry or rice wine vinegar
1 tsp. lemon juice
grated lemon peel from one lemon

1/4 cup chopped black Kalamata olives
1/4 cup diced pimiento or roasted red pepper
1/4 cup coarsely grated carrot
2 tbs. minced parsley
salt and freshly ground black pepper

Spray rice cooker container with nonstick spray. Add rice, bouillon cube and water. Cover and cook until rice cooker turns off. Allow to steam for 5 to 10 minutes. Pour cooked rice into a large mixing bowl and fluff with a fork. Immediately toss with olive oil to keep rice grains from sticking together. Allow to cool a few minutes. Stir in wine vinegar, lemon juice and lemon peel. Add remaining ingredients. Spray a 4- to 5-cup mold with nonstick spray. Press rice mixture into mold. Cover and let stand in a cool place 1 to 2 hours to develop flavors. To unmold, place serving plate over mold and invert. Fill center with chicken salad or another vegetable.

LEMON, CAPER AND PINE NUT SALAD

This is a bright lemon- and dill-flavored salad which is delicious with fish and chicken dishes. It can be pressed into a ring mold for an elegant presentation.

1 cup long-grain rice
1 can (14¼ oz.) chicken broth
2 tbs. full-flavored olive oil
rind from 1 lemon
1 tbs. lemon juice
1 tbs. rice wine vinegar
2 tbs. capers, chopped coarsely if
  large

½ tsp. dried dill weed
¼ cup minced parsley
salt and freshly ground pepper
¼ cup toasted pine nuts or slivered
  almonds

Spray rice cooker container with nonstick spray. Add rice and chicken broth. Cover and cook until rice cooker turns off. Allow to steam for 5 to 10 minutes. Spoon rice into a large mixing bowl, fluff with a fork and add olive oil to keep rice grains from sticking together. Allow rice to cool a few minutes and add remaining ingredients, tossing with 2 forks. Rice can be served hot, room temperature, or refrigerated for several hours before serving.

VARIATION
Stir ⅓ cup plain yogurt into rice before placing in a mold.

SMOKED SALMON AND
NEW POTATO SALAD

Small new potatoes and smoked salmon dressed with dill and yogurt make a nice first course or luncheon salad.

12 oz. small new potatoes, unpeeled
1 tbs. sweet hot mustard
2 tbs. lowfat yogurt
½ tsp. dried dill, or 1 tbs. fresh dill, chopped
1 tbs. parsley, minced
salt and freshly ground pepper
1 to 2 oz. thinly sliced smoked salmon, cut into 1-inch squares

Steam potatoes in rice cooker according to directions on page 106. When cool enough to handle, slice each potato into quarters and place in a bowl. Mix together sweet hot mustard, yogurt, dill and parsley. Gently toss with potatoes; season with salt and pepper to taste. Add smoked salmon pieces. Refrigerate until ready to serve. This can be made a day ahead.

ITALIAN-STYLE TUNA MAYONNAISE

Makes 2 cups

*This makes a creamy sauce perfect for dressing cooked chicken cubes, **Steamed Turkey Tenderloins**, page 99, spreading over a platter of thinly sliced cooked pork or veal, or to accompany sliced new potatoes or green beans.*

1 egg
2 tbs. lemon juice
½ tsp. salt
dash Tabasco

1 cup light olive oil
1 can (6-½ oz.) tuna with oil
4 flat anchovies, rinsed and chopped
generous amount of white pepper

Place egg, lemon juice, salt and Tabasco in a blender container or food processor bowl; process 30 to 45 seconds. At low speed slowly pour in oil. When mixture starts to thicken, add tuna, oil, anchovies and white pepper; process until smooth. Refrigerate until ready to serve.

SERVING SUGGESTION

Combine 2 cups cooked chicken cubes with ½ cup of *Italian-Style Tuna Mayonnaise*. Fill center of *Party Rice Ring*, page 59, and garnish with black olives and red pepper strips.

DELI RICE SALAD

Take this salad for lunch. It packs well and goes together quickly if you have some cooked rice.

2 cups cooked long-grain rice
½ cup drained kidney or garbanzo
 beans
4 oz. turkey salami, or smoked ham,
 cut in slivers

4 oz. smoked Gouda or Provolone,
 cut in small dice
2 tbs. finely chopped red onion
2 tbs. finely chopped fresh parsley
¼ tsp. dried red pepper flakes
salt and freshly ground pepper

VINAIGRETTE
¼ cup light olive oil
1 tbs. cider vinegar
1 tsp. Dijon mustard

½ tsp. Italian herb seasoning
salt and freshly ground pepper

Combine salad ingredients in a large bowl. Whisk vinaigrette until well combined, pour over salad and toss with two forks. Refrigerate for 1 to 2 hours before serving.

NEW POTATO SALAD

This is delicious as an accompaniment for grilled meats or paired with other salads on those nights when it is too hot to cook. Fresh tarragon or basil instead of thyme is a nice variation. The potatoes are fragile so dress each layer as it is sliced.

1 lb. small new potatoes, unpeeled
2 tbs. full-flavored olive oil
2 tsp. sherry wine vinegar or rice
  wine vinegar
1/4 tsp. sugar

leaves from two sprigs of fresh thyme
1 to 2 small green onions, minced
1 tbs. parsley, minced
salt and freshly ground black pepper

Cook potatoes in rice cooker (see page 106). Combine olive oil, wine vinegar and sugar. When potatoes are cool enough to handle, slice each potato in about 4 slices. Place a layer of sliced potatoes in a small serving bowl, sprinkle with fresh thyme leaves, parsley, onions, salt and pepper, and drizzle with a small amount of olive oil mixture. Continue with another layer of potatoes, herbs and dressing until all potatoes and dressing have been used. Gently pour out dressing which has accumulated in bottom of bowl, and pour over salad again. Serve warm or at room temperature. If salad is refrigerated, allow it to warm a little before serving.

RICE SALAD NIÇOISE

Servings: 3 to 4

Fresh cooked rice with lemon makes a great variation on the classic potato for a salad Niçoise. Steam the green beans in the rice cooker and then cook the rice for the salad. Rice salads are better if made with freshly cooked rice, or if refrigerated, allow them to stand at room temperature for a short time before serving.

1 lb. small green beans, stemmed, cooked (see page 114)
1 cup long-grain rice
1 tbs. butter
1 tbs. lemon juice
½ tsp. salt
2 cups water
2 to 3 tbs. minced parsley, fresh or dried
2 tbs. capers, drained and rinsed
2 fresh, ripe tomatoes, peeled, seeded and cut into quarters
2 hard boiled eggs, peeled, cut into quarters
about 20 olives, Niçoise or Kalamata
2 cans (6½ oz.) white chunk tuna, well drained

DRESSING

1/3 cup full-flavored olive oil
2 tbs. red wine vinegar
1 tsp. Dijon mustard
3 to 4 fresh thyme sprigs, leaves only
1 to 2 anchovies, finely chopped
salt and freshly ground pepper

Spray rice cooker container with nonstick spray. Add rice, butter, lemon juice, salt and 1¾ cups water. Cover and cook until rice cooker turns off. Steam 10 minutes, covered. Whisk dressing ingredients together in a small bowl to make an emulsion. Pour rice into a mixing bowl; add parsley, capers and about ½ of the dressing. Stir and let cool. Coat cooked green beans with a little dressing.

To assemble: Use a large platter or assemble salads on individual plates. Mound rice in center of platter or divide among 3 to 4 plates. Arrange tomato wedges, eggs, green beans and olives around rice. Arrange drained tuna chunks around rice. Drizzle vegetables and tuna with salad dressing. Serve at room temperature.

CURRIED RICE AND CHICKEN SALAD

Servings: 4

*This makes a great luncheon dish. Arrange the beautiful orange rice on a platter, top with cooked chicken pieces, fresh cilantro leaves and serve with **Cucumber Raita**, page 65.*

2 tbs. butter
1 tsp. curry powder
1 tsp. dried onion flakes
1 cup long-grain rice
2 cups chicken broth
½ tsp. cumin
¼ tsp. dried dill
½ tsp. salt
¼ cup raisins, golden or dark
2 cups cooked chicken cut into 1-inch pieces
⅓ cup dry roasted peanuts
fresh cilantro leaves

Spray rice cooker container with nonstick spray. Place butter in container, turn rice cooker on and melt butter. Add curry powder and cook 1 to 2 minutes to bring out flavor. Add onion flakes and rice; stir to coat the rice. Add chicken broth, cumin, dill and salt. Cover and cook for 15 minutes. Add raisins, cover and continue to cook until rice cooker shuts off. Allow rice to steam for 10 minutes before removing cover.

Pour cooked rice onto a serving platter or bowl, and allow to cool for a few minutes. When rice is barely warm, arrange chicken pieces over rice, spoon a little *Cucumber Raita* over the chicken. Sprinkle with peanuts and fresh cilantro leaves. Serve at room temperature with more *Cucumber Raita* and a chutney, if desired.

CUCUMBER RAITA

2 cups peeled, seeded, coarsely grated cucumber	1 tsp. salt
	freshly ground pepper
1 cup plain lowfat yogurt	¼ cup fresh chopped cilantro or
2 tsp. cumin	sweet basil leaves

Combine ingredients in a small bowl, cover and refrigerate 1 to 2 hours before serving.

SAN JUAN BLACK BEAN
AND RICE SALAD

Servings: 4

This hearty salad includes some Caribbean flavors. Feta cheese was used because it is more widely available than queso fresco (Mexican-style fresh cheese). Serve with a fresh fruit platter of melon, mango and pineapple slices.

2 cups cooked rice
1 can (15 oz.) black beans, drained
   and rinsed
1/4 cup diced roasted red peppers

6 to 8 black Kalamata olives, pitted
   and chopped
3 oz. feta cheese, crumbled
fresh cilantro

DRESSING

1/4 cup full-flavored olive oil
1 tbs. red wine vinegar
1 tbs. lemon juice

1 tsp. Dijon mustard
salt and generous amounts of freshly
   ground black pepper

Combine rice, beans, red peppers and olive pieces in a serving bowl. Whisk dressing ingredients together in a small bowl and toss with rice. Sprinkle with feta cheese and fresh cilantro. Serve at room temperature.

QUICK RICE SALAD

Use your favorite prepared salad dressing and mix it with hot cooked rice for an instant, slightly piquant side dish. Try Italian, ranch or other zesty dressing for variation. Serve in lettuce or radicchio cups and garnish with pieces of fresh tomato, black olives, cilantro leaves or fresh parsley.

1 cup uncooked long-grain rice
1¾ cups water
½ tsp. salt
½ cup prepared salad dressing

Spray the rice cooker container with nonstick cooking spray. Add rice, water and salt. Cover and cook until rice cooker shuts off. Allow to steam 8 to 10 minutes. Spoon rice into a serving bowl and add salad dressing, tossing to mix well. Let cool before spooning into lettuce cups.

HEARTY MAIN COURSES

Beans, lentils or a little meat round out rice-based dishes to make delicious main courses. Lentils cook as well as rice in the rice cooker, but require a little more liquid and time. *Basque-Style Rice with Clams*, *Brown Rice with Green Chiles* and *Arroz con Pollo* are cooked directly in the rice cooker so there is only one pot to clean. Chicken noodle soup mix is added to rice in *Savory Sausage and Rice* for a flavorful, spicy entrée. We include a tasty *Rice with Lentils* and an *East Indian Rice* which uses split pink dal found in markets that sell ethnic foods.

A tip: Immediately after you remove the dish from the rice cooker, pour some water into the cooker container for easier cleanup later.

INDIVIDUAL BROWN RICE MEAT LOAVES   Servings: 6

Fold leftover cooked brown rice into your meat loaf mixture for added moistness and texture. For quicker cooking, form into individual meat loaves.

2 tbs. olive oil
1 large onion, chopped
½ lb. mushrooms, coarsely chopped
1 large garlic clove, minced
2 tbs. dried sweet pepper flakes or
  ¼ cup diced fresh red or green pepper
1½ lbs. ground meat (beef, pork, or
  turkey or combination)

2 eggs
1½ cups cooked brown rice
1 tbs. Worcestershire sauce
1 tbs. Dijon mustard
2 tbs. tomato paste
1 tsp. salt
freshly ground pepper
dash red pepper flakes

Heat oil in a large skillet. Sauté onions 2 to 3 minutes. Add mushrooms, garlic and sweet pepper flakes or fresh peppers. Continue to cook 3 to 4 minutes. Allow to cool slightly before adding to meat and egg mixture.

Preheat oven to 350°. Combine remaining ingredients; add onion mushroom mixture. Form into 6 round or oval shaped loaves. Place in a 9-x-13-pan or other pan with sides. Bake 45 or 50 minutes, or until internal temperature reaches 160°.

A tip: Lining the pan with foil eases cleanup.

BASQUE-STYLE RICE AND CLAMS

Servings: 3 to 4

Serve with a crisp salad, or fill individual shells or au gratin dishes for a first course. Fresh clams make an attractive garnish but the dish is delicious without them.

2 cans (6½ oz. each) chopped clams
1 bottle (8 oz.) clam juice
3 tbs. full-flavored olive oil
½ cup chopped onion
2 garlic cloves, minced
1 cup uncooked medium grain rice
⅓ cup finely chopped parsley
1 large tomato, peeled, seeded, chopped
pinch of saffron threads, optional
½ tsp. salt
6 to 8 fresh clams in shells, scrubbed, optional
dash red pepper flakes
½ cup diced cooked ham or frozen green peas

Drain clams and reserve juice. Combine reserved clam juice with bottle of clam juice plus enough water to make 2¼ cups total liquid. Spray rice cooker container with nonstick cooking spray. Add olive oil. When hot, sauté onions and garlic over low heat 3 to 4 minutes to soften onion. Pour in clam juice, rice, onion, parsley, tomato, saffron, salt, fresh clams and red pepper flakes. Cover and cook until liquid evaporates and rice cooker turns off. Immediately lift lid, remove cooked clams in the shells, and quickly stir in chopped clams, ham or peas and red pepper strips. Cover and allow to steam for an additional 10 minutes. Serve immediately. Garnish with whole clams in shell.

VARIATION

To serve as a first course, fill individual ovenproof serving dishes with rice and clam mixture. Sprinkle with buttered fresh bread crumbs or Parmesan cheese. Place under broiler for a few minutes to brown lightly. Makes 6 to 8 first course servings.

SAVORY SAUSAGE AND RICE

This is a favorite rainy night dinner. Serve with a crisp green salad, garlic bread, and a red zinfandel wine.

1 cup uncooked long-grain rice
1 pkg. (2 oz.) chicken noodle soup mix
3½ cups water
1 lb. mild or hot bulk sausage
1 cup onion, chopped
1 fresh green or red pepper, peeled, diced

1 tbs. dried parsley
2 fresh tomatoes, peeled, seeded, chopped
salt and freshly ground pepper
grated Parmesan cheese

Spray the rice cooker container with nonstick spray. Add rice, chicken noodle soup mix and water. Cover and cook until rice cooker shuts off. While rice is cooking, brown sausage in a nonstick skillet, crumbling it into small pieces as it cooks. Remove sausage to a strainer and drain. Return about 2 tbs. of sausage drippings to skillet. Sauté onion and red pepper for 5 to 6 minutes until soft but not browned. When rice cooker turns off, carefully remove cover and quickly stir in cooked meat, onion mixture, dried parsley and fresh tomatoes. Cover and allow to continue steaming for 10 minutes. Spoon into a warm serving bowl and serve immediately. Pass Parmesan cheese, if desired.

BROWN RICE AND GREEN CHILES

Servings: 2 to 3

The combination of rice, green chiles and cheese has always been a family favorite. The brown rice adds a nice texture and flavor.

1 cup medium-grain brown rice
3 cups water
1 tbs. dried onion flakes
½ tsp. salt
1 can (4 oz.) green chiles, drained and diced
¾ cup grated sharp cheddar cheese
1 fresh tomato, peeled, seeded, chopped
fresh cilantro for garnish

Spray rice cooker container with nonstick spray. Add rice, water, onion flakes and salt. Cover and cook until rice cooker turns off. Carefully remove the lid and quickly stir in green chiles, cheese and tomato pieces. Cover and allow to steam for 10 minutes. Spoon into a warm serving dish, garnish with fresh cilantro and serve immediately.

ARROZ CON POLLO

Servings: 4

Succulent morsels of chicken are cooked with rice and spices to make a delicious supper or hearty lunch. Dried herbs and vegetables make this dish go together quickly.

6 chicken thighs, skin removed,
  boned, cut into 8 pieces each or
  1 lb. boneless, skinless thighs
  cut into 1-inch pieces
3 tbs. full-flavored olive oil
1 red pepper, peeled, seeded, chopped
1½ cups medium-grain rice
2 tbs. dried onion flakes
1 tsp. dehydrated minced garlic

2 tbs. freeze-dried green pepper
1 tbs. dried parsley
2 tsp. Spanish paprika
3 cups chicken stock
1½ cups canned tomato pieces with
  juice
salt and freshly ground pepper
pinch of saffron, optional

Spray rice cooker container with nonstick spray. Heat olive oil in rice container and sauté chicken pieces 2 to 3 minutes to brown lightly. Add red pepper and rice. Stir to coat rice. Add remaining ingredients, stir, cover and cook until rice cooker shuts off. Carefully remove cover and stir rice. Cover and allow to steam for 10 minutes before serving.

RICE WITH LENTILS

This hearty dish is punctuated with sun-dried tomatoes. The brown lentils take longer to cook than the rice, so they are cooked a few minutes alone before adding the rice. Serve with a fresh fruit or green salad, crisp cheese bread, and a red zinfandel wine.

½ cup lentils, picked over and washed
3 tbs. full-flavored olive oil
3 cups beef or chicken broth
2 tbs. dehydrated onion
½ tsp. dried garlic
2 tbs. dried parsley
1 cup medium-grain rice

½ tsp. salt
1 tsp. ground cumin
¼ tsp. red pepper flakes
¼ cup diced sun-dried tomatoes (not packed in oil)
1 medium fresh tomato, peeled, seeded, chopped for garnish

Spray rice cooker container with nonstick cooking spray. Add lentils, olive oil and beef or chicken broth. Cover and cook 15 minutes. Add remaining ingredients except fresh tomato pieces and continue to cook until rice cooker shuts off. Carefully remove cover, quickly stir and recover. Allow to steam for 10 minutes before serving. Spoon into a serving bowl and top with chopped fresh tomato. Serve immediately.

HARVEST MEDLEY

Eggplant, tomatoes and garbanzo beans are cooked with rice for a flavorful easy lunch or supper. Serve with some crunchy garlic bread and a green salad.

1 cup diced eggplant
1 can (14¼ oz.) tomato pieces with juice
1 can (15½ oz.) garbanzo beans with juice
½ cup uncooked short-grain rice
2 tbs. dried onion flakes

¼ tsp. minced dried garlic
½ tsp. dried oregano
½ tsp. dried sweet basil
⅛ tsp. red pepper flakes, or to taste
salt and freshly ground pepper
1 tbs. full-flavored olive oil

Peel and cut eggplant into ½-inch cubes. Place on a microwavable plate and microwave on high for 2 minutes. Spray the rice cooker container with nonstick spray. Pour juice from tomatoes and garbanzo beans into a measuring cup; add enough water to make 1⅓ cups liquid. Pour liquid into rice cooker and add eggplant and all remaining ingredients. Cover and cook until rice cooker turns off, about 20 minutes. Carefully remove cover and spoon vegetable mixture into a warm serving bowl.

EAST INDIAN RICE

The pretty pink colored dal, or split lentils, found in markets that sell ethnic foods, are combined with rice and spices for a tasty side dish.

½ cup dal, picked over and washed
2 tbs. olive oil
1 cup medium-grain rice
2½ cups chicken stock
2 tbs. dehydrated onion
¼ tsp. dried garlic
2 tbs. dried parsley

1 tsp. cumin
¼ tsp. red pepper flakes
salt and freshly ground pepper
2 fresh tomatoes, peeled, seeded,
   chopped for garnish
fresh cilantro for garnish

Spray rice cooker container with nonstick cooking spray. Add all ingredients except for fresh tomatoes and cilantro garnish. Cover and cook until rice cooker shuts off. Carefully remove the cover, stir and recover. Allow to steam for another 10 minutes before serving. Place in a serving bowl, garnish with fresh tomato and cilantro and serve.

If you have leftovers, use them to stuff hollowed-out fresh tomatoes, and steam for 5 minutes to heat through.

SAVORY LENTILS

Lentils, like rice and pasta, make a wonderful base for almost any combination of spices and flavors. This is a quick and easy side dish.

1 tbs. full-flavored olive oil
½ tsp. curry powder
1 tsp. cumin
1 cup brown lentils, picked over
  and washed
2½ cups water

1 (14 oz.) can tomato pieces
  with juice
2 tbs. dehydrated onion
2 tbs. dried parsley
1 tsp. dried celery flakes
salt and freshly ground pepper

Spray rice cooker container with nonstick cooking spray. Turn rice cooker on; add olive oil, curry powder and cumin. Cook for 2 to 3 minutes to bring out curry and cumin flavors. Add remaining ingredients, cover and cook until rice cooker shuts off. Stir once midway through cooking. Carefully remove cover and stir. Recover and allow to steam for 10 minutes before serving.

SEAFOOD

Shellfish and other seafood only need the quickest cooking or steaming to bring out their delicious flavors. *Shrimp Cooked in Beer* and *Steamed Clams* are classic preparations easily done in the rice cooker. Shrimp and salmon steamed with aromatic flavorings go together quickly and fit right in with today's healthful eating patterns. Steam your favorite fish in one of these marinades for dinner tonight.

A small artichoke holder or a platform made out of an 8-oz. can with both ends cut out of it makes a good spacer to hold the plate above the steaming water. For quick cleanup, be sure to spray the plate you are steaming with non-stick cooking spray before placing the fish and marinade on it.

SHRIMP COOKED IN BEER

This is an easy dish for informal entertaining, and if you have any left over, refrigerate and eat it for lunch the next day.

medium size shrimp in the shell
beer
dash red pepper flakes
1 tsp. dried celery flakes
salt

With scissors, cut shrimp shells down the back. Pull out the dark vein and rinse with water. Spray rice cooker container with nonstick spray and add shrimp. Pour in enough beer to cover shrimp. Add remaining ingredients. Turn rice cooker on, no need to cover, and bring beer to a boil. Stir once or twice. Shrimp are done when they turn a bright pink, about 3 to 4 minutes. Immediately pour shrimp into a strainer and then into a serving bowl. Serve warm, cold or at room temperature with lots of napkins, a bowl for shells, and *Aïoli*, page 126, or cocktail sauce.

SALMON FILLETS IN WHITE WINE AND MUSTARD

Servings: 2

Salmon fillets steamed with white wine and dill make an elegant dinner for two. Serve with fresh sweet corn and a salad of tender greens.

2 salmon fillets, about 6 to 7 oz. each
1 tsp. Dijon mustard
2 tbs. white wine
¼ tsp. dried dill weed, or 1 tsp. fresh
  chopped dill

¼ tsp. sugar
1 green onion, thinly sliced
1 cup water

Make two foil boats, each just a little larger than fillets. Rub salmon with mustard and place in foil boats, skin side down. Combine white wine, dill and sugar. Pour over fish and top with thinly sliced onion. Spray rice cooker container and steamer plate with nonstick spray. Add 1 cup water to rice cooker and a small rack or can to support steamer plate. Place foil boats on steamer plate, cover rice cooker and steam about 10 minutes, depending on thickness of fish. Check fish at 8 minutes. Do not overcook. Carefully lift out of cooker, remove foil and serve on a warm plate. Pour cooking juices over fish, if desired.

SALMON STEAMED IN GRAPE LEAVES

Servings: 2

Grape leaves are a flavorful wrapper for fish or chicken.

2 salmon fillets, 6 to 7 oz. each
4 to 6 grape leaves in brine, rinsed
  with cold water and dried
full-flavored olive oil

¼ tsp. dried dill weed
2 lemon slices
1 cup water

Make two foil boats, each just a little larger than fish fillet. Fold thin part of fish under to make a more uniform piece of fish. Drizzle each fillet with oil, sprinkle with dill and place 1 slice of lemon on top of each fillet. Cut protruding stems from of grape leaves. Arrange 2 or 3 leaves together, depending on size. Place fish in the middle and bring edges of leaves together to enclose fish completely. Place grape leaf packages in foil boats.

Spray rice cooker container and steamer plate with nonstick spray. Add 1 cup water and a small rack or can to hold steamer plate. Place foil packages on steamer plate, cover rice cooker and cook about 10 minutes, depending on size and thickness of fish. Start checking fish at 7 or 8 minutes. Do not overcook. Carefully remove fish packages to a plate, and allow each diner to unwrap grape leaves, or remove grape leaves and present fish with slice of lemon on top.

SALMON WITH HOISIN SAUCE

Servings: 2

The sweetness of the hoisin sauce compliments the salmon. Hoisin sauce is available in Asian markets and many supermarkets.

2 salmon fillets, 6 to 7 oz. each
1 tsp. hoisin sauce
2 tsp. rice wine vinegar
1/2 tsp. sesame oil

2 tsp. soy sauce
1/4 tsp. grated fresh ginger
3 to 4 fresh cilantro leaves

Make two foil boats, each just a little larger than fish fillet. Fold thin part of fish under to make a more uniform piece of fish. Combine remaining ingredients except for cilantro leaves and spread on 2 salmon pieces. Place each fillet, skin side down, in a foil boat and top with cilantro leaves.

Spray rice cooker container and steamer plate with nonstick spray. Add 1 cup water and small rack or platform to hold plate. Place foil packages on steamer plate, cover rice cooker and cook about 10 minutes, depending on size and thickness of fish. Start checking fish at 7 or 8 minutes. Do not overcook. Carefully lift fish from foil and place on serving plates. Pour over some cooking juices if desired, and serve. Garnish with fresh cilantro leaves.

CHINESE-STYLE STEAMED ROCK COD

Servings: 2

Rock cod or other firm-fleshed fish with a simple marinade makes a savory steamed entrée for dinner.

2 rock cod fillets, about 4 to 6 oz. each
1 tbs. soy sauce
¼ tsp. sesame oil
1 small garlic clove, minced
1 tsp. fresh ginger, minced
pinch white pepper
1 tbs. rice wine vinegar
2 green onions, white part only, slivered
5 to 6 slivered snow peas
fresh cilantro leaves
1 cup water

Place 2 fish fillets on a plate which will allow about ½-inch circulation around it in rice cooker. Fold thin ends of fish under to make a fillet of uniform thickness. Mix together soy sauce, sesame oil, garlic, ginger, white pepper and rice wine vinegar. Pour over fish fillets. Top with slivered onions and snow peas. Cover plate with plastic wrap. Spray rice cooker container with nonstick cooking spray. Pour water in bottom of cooker and put in a small rack or 8-oz. can with both ends cut out of it to support plate. Cover cooker, bring to a boil and carefully lower plate with fish onto rack. Cover and time cooking of fish. Allow approximately 7 to 8 minutes for fish to cook. Do not overcook. The fish is done when it flakes or feels firm to the touch. Carefully remove plate from rice cooker with a plate lifter. Uncover and remove to serving plates. Garnish with fresh cilantro leaves. Serve immediately.

VARIATION

Almost any fish can be used in this preparation. Consider using red snapper, halibut or salmon fillets.

STEAMED SHRIMP DIJON

Servings: 1 to 2

Shrimp only need a delicate marinade and 4 to 5 minutes steaming to make a perfect appetizer for 2, or an entrée for 1.

4 oz. small shrimp, peeled, deveined (51-60 per pound)

MARINADE
1 tsp. dry sherry
1 tsp. olive oil
1 tsp. Dijon mustard

1 tsp. lemon juice
¼ tsp. dried tarragon

Combine marinade ingredients in a small bowl. Coat shrimp with marinade and let stand 10 minutes. Spray rice cooker container with nonstick spray. Pour 1½ cups water into rice cooker and place in it a small rack or can with both ends cut out of it to support plate. Cover and bring to a boil. With nonstick spray, spray a small plate that will fit into cooker with about ½-inch clearance for steam circulation. Arrange marinated shrimp in single layer on the plate and cover with plastic wrap. When water in cooker comes to a boil, carefully place plate on plate support, cover and steam for 4 to 5 minutes, until shrimp are pink and firm to the touch. Carefully remove plate with a plate lifter and remove plastic wrap. Serve immediately.

CANTONESE-STYLE STEAMED SHRIMP
Servings: 1 to 2

This is a traditional-style soy sauce-based marinade. The lemon rind and juice give a little flavor spark. Makes a great appetizer for two or an individual entrée with some rice and a vegetable.

4 oz. shrimp, peeled, deveined (about 51 to 60 per pound)

MARINADE
1 tsp. soy sauce
1 tsp. sesame oil
1 tsp. lemon juice

1 tsp. lemon rind
2 green onions, white part only, cut
  into long slivers

Mix marinade ingredients together and coat shrimp. Allow to stand about 10 minutes. Spray a small plate that will fit into rice cooker container with nonstick spray and place marinated shrimp in single layer on plate. Cover with plastic wrap. Spray rice cooker container with nonstick spray and in it place a small rack or can with both ends cut out of it for a plate platform. Pour in 2 cups water and bring water to a boil. Carefully remove rice cooker cover, and using a plate lifter, place plate with shrimp on plate holder. Cover and steam 4 to 5 minutes until shrimp are pink and firm. Carefully remove plate from cooker with a plate lifter, remove plastic wrap and serve immediately as an appetizer or entrée.

STEAMED CLAMS

Allow an hour or so to soak the clams so they release the sand. These are delicious with some of the broth or a little melted butter and lemon juice for dipping.

1½ lbs. clams in the shell
1 cup water or white wine

Wash clams under running water and place in a bowl covered with 1 quart of cold water and 1 tbs. salt. Allow to stand an hour so clams release sand. Drain and rinse. Place clams in a steamer basket. Spray rice cooker container with nonstick spray. Place steamer basket in cooker with water or wine. Cover and cook 8 to 10 minutes until clams have opened. Discard any clams that do not open. Remove clams to a bowl. If desired, continue to cook broth 3 to 4 minutes to reduce it, carefully pour off broth, leaving sand in bottom of container, and use it for a dipping sauce.

POULTRY

Boneless pieces of chicken or turkey steam quickly in the rice cooker. Just add some aromatic herbs, wine or broth and you have a healthful entrée. Pesto, mustard, or the Asian soy sauce and ginger combination all complement poultry.

CHICKEN BREASTS TERIYAKI

Servings: 2

Boneless, skinless chicken breasts or turkey cutlets are marinated and cooked in a teriyaki sauce. Use a bottled sauce or the recipe given below.

2 boneless, skinless chicken breasts
2 tbs. soy sauce
1 tbs. sugar
1 tsp. sesame oil
1 small garlic clove, minced

½ tsp. grated fresh ginger
1 green onion, white part only, cut
  into slivers
1 cup water

Combine soy sauce, sugar, sesame oil, garlic and ginger with chicken breasts and marinate 10 to 15 minutes. Place chicken breasts and marinade on a plate sprayed with nonstick cooking spray that is just large enough to fit into rice cooker with about ½-inch clearance for steam circulation. Top with slivered onion and cover plate with plastic wrap.

Add water to rice cooker container and in it place a small rack or 8-oz. can with both ends cut out in cooker for a pate platform. Place plate on rack, cover rice cooker and bring to a boil. Steam chicken for about 10 minutes after water has come to a boil. Cook until chicken is firm to touch. Carefully remove plate from rice cooker with a plate lifter. Serve chicken breasts on plates with a spoonful of marinade.

PARISIAN-STYLE CHICKEN BREASTS

Servings: 2

Boned chicken breasts make a wonderful fast and savory dinner entrée.

2 boned, skinned chicken breasts
2 tbs. butter
1 tbs. minced shallots
¼ cup dry white wine
salt and freshly ground pepper
dash Tabasco sauce

1 cup water
1 fresh tomato, peeled, seeded, chopped
5 to 6 fresh sweet basil leaves, finely shredded

Place boned chicken breasts on a plate sprayed with nonstick cooking spray just large enough to fit into rice cooker with about ½-inch clearance for steam circulation. In a small skillet, melt butter and sauté shallots for 1 to 2 minutes to soften. Pour in white wine, turn heat to high and reduce for 1 minute.

Spray rice cooker container with nonstick spray and add 1 cup water. Place a small rack or an 8 oz. can with both ends cut out to support plate in cooker. Pour shallot mixture over chicken, cover with plastic wrap, and place plate on rack. Cover rice cooker, bring to a boil and cook about 10 minutes, or until chicken is firm to the touch and cooked. Carefully remove from rice cooker, take off plastic wrap and place on serving plates. Garnish with tomato pieces and shredded basil leaves.

CHICKEN BREASTS WITH PESTO

Servings: 2

Homemade pesto or pesto paste from a tube makes a zesty marinade for chicken breasts. Garnish with Parmesan cheese and toasted pine nuts.

2 boneless, skinned chicken breasts
2 tsp. pesto paste
salt and freshly ground pepper
1 cup water

2 tbs. toasted pine nuts
1 fresh tomato, peeled, seeded, chopped
grated Parmesan cheese

Place chicken breasts on a plate, sprayed with nonstick spray, just large enough to fit into rice cooker with about ½-inch clearance for steam circulation. Spread pesto over top of breasts; season with salt and pepper. Cover plate with plastic wrap. Spray rice cooker container with nonstick spray. Add 1 cup water. Place a rack or an 8-oz. can with both ends cut out of it to support plate in rice cooker. Place plate on platform, cover rice cooker, bring to a boil and steam for about 10 minutes after water has come to a boil. Cook until chicken is firm to the touch. Carefully remove plate from rice cooker with a plate lifter. Serve chicken breasts on plates; garnish each serving with pine nuts, chopped tomato and a spoonful of Parmesan cheese. Serve immediately.

DIJON CHICKEN BREASTS

Servings: 2

A simple marinade of Dijon mustard and yogurt makes a quick savory chicken entrée. This makes a delicious hot toasted sandwich, as well.

2 boneless, skinless chicken breasts
2 tsp. Dijon mustard
2 tsp. plain yogurt

salt and freshly ground pepper
1 tsp. dried chives
1 cup water

Place chicken breasts on a plate, sprayed with nonstick spray, just large enough to fit into rice cooker container with about ½-inch clearance for steam circulation. Mix together mustard, yogurt, salt and pepper. Spread over chicken breasts and sprinkle with chives. Cover chicken on plate with plastic wrap. Spray rice cooker container with nonstick spray. Place a small rack or an 8-oz. can with both ends cut out of it in cooker container to support plate. Pour in water and place plate on platform. Cover rice cooker, bring to a boil and cook chicken for about 10 minutes after water has come to a boil. Chicken is done when firm to the touch. Carefully remove plate from rice cooker with a plate lifter and remove plastic wrap. Place chicken breasts on serving plates. Serve immediately.

CHICKEN SEAFOOD ROLLS

Makes 3 rolls

Chicken breasts are lightly flattened and spread with a creamy shrimp and scallop mousse, then rolled up and steamed. They make a delicious cold appetizer with red pepper or caper-flavored mayonnaise, or serve them hot with **Clam Sauce**, *page 96.*

3 chicken breasts, skinned and boned
1½ oz. small raw shrimp, peeled, deveined
1½ oz. bay scallops, washed, white muscle removed
1 tbs. heavy cream
2 tsp. dried parsley flakes or 1 tbs. fresh
1 tsp. dried or fresh chives
salt and generous amount of white pepper

Place each chicken breast between 2 pieces of waxed paper. Starting in center, pound into an even flat thickness with a poultry or meat pounder. Place remaining ingredients in a food processor bowl and process 2 to 3 minutes until very smooth. Spread seafood mixture over each chicken breast and roll into a sausage shape about 2 inches in diameter. Tuck in sides as you roll to make a neat package. Wrap each breast in a double thickness of plastic wrap and tie ends of wrap with string. Place on a plate sprayed with nonstick spray that will fit into rice cooker leaving ½-inch circulation space.

Spray rice cooker container with nonstick spray. Place a steamer rack or platform in cooker and put the plate of chicken rolls on rack. Cover rice cooker, bring to a boil and steam for about 20 to 25 minutes after water boils. Rolls are done when firm to the touch. Carefully remove rolls from rice cooker; allow to cool 1 to 2 minutes before unwrapping if serving hot. If serving cold, leave in wrap and refrigerate for several hours or overnight before slicing and serving. To serve hot, slice into 7 to 8 slices and slightly overlap them on individual plates. Spoon some sauce over chicken and serve.

To serve cold, after refrigerating, slice into 8 to 10 slices and place on crackers or small toasts with a dollop of flavored mayonnaise.

CLAM SAUCE FOR CHICKEN SEAFOOD ROLLS

Here is a flavorful quick sauce to serve with the steamed chicken rolls.

1 tbs. butter
4 green onions, white part only, thinly sliced
8 oz. clam juice
salt and freshly ground pepper
2 tsp. cornstarch dissolved in 1 tbs. cold water

Melt butter and sauté onion 1 to 2 minutes until it softens. Pour in clam juice, add salt and pepper, and bring to a boil. Pour in some of the cornstarch mixture and cook 1 to 2 minutes until mixture thickens. Add just enough cornstarch to bring sauce to a nice pouring consistency.

ROAST CHICKEN WITH WILD BLEND APRICOT STUFFING

Lundberg Farms produces a blend of brown, sweet, Wehani and black Japonica rices which makes a savory side dish or is a delicious stuffing base. Use to stuff 4 Cornish game hens instead of a large chicken.

1 cup Wild Blend rice
2¼ cups water or chicken stock

1 tbs. butter
salt

STUFFING

2 tbs. butter
½ cup onion, chopped
½ cup diced dried apricots
1 tsp. dried celery flakes
1 tbs. dried parsley flakes

1 egg
salt and pepper
2 cups cooked and cooled Wild
  Blend rice

Cook rice in rice cooker and allow to cool. Preheat oven to 375°. Sauté onion in butter 3 to 4 minutes until onion softens and is translucent. Combine onion and remaining ingredients and stuff a 4½ to 5 lb. chicken. Truss chicken and place on rack in roasting pan. Roast for about 1¾ hours, depending on size and temperature of chicken (185°). Allow chicken to stand for 15 to 20 minutes before carving.

CHICKEN WITH ORANGE AND BLACK BEAN RICE

Servings: 4

This spicy dish with wonderful flavors of orange, black beans, garlic and ginger was inspired by a recipe of Ken Hom's. Dried salted black beans and chili bean paste with garlic are available in Asian markets and in some supermarkets.

1 tbs. vegetable oil
2 garlic cloves, minced
2 tbs. salted black beans, rinsed, chopped
1 tbs. fresh grated ginger
1 cup uncooked long-grain rice
grated zest from two oranges
1 cup orange juice

1 cup chicken broth
3 tbs. soy sauce
½ tsp. chili bean paste with garlic, or substitute ¼ tsp. red pepper flakes, or 6-8 drops Tabasco
5 to 6 chicken thighs, boned, skinned and cut into 6 to 7 pieces each

Spray rice cooker container with nonstick cooking spray. Heat vegetable oil in rice cooker container and add garlic, black beans and ginger. Cook, stirring 1 to 2 minutes until garlic and black beans release some of their flavor. Add rice and stir to combine. Add remaining ingredients, cover and cook until rice cooker shuts off. Stir once during cooking. Allow rice to steam for about 10 minutes before serving.

STEAMED TURKEY TENDERLOINS

*Cooked turkey tenderloins make great sandwiches and salads. They steam in about 25 minutes and can be done ahead and refrigerated. A general rule is to steam for 15 minutes per 1-inch thickness. After the tenderloins have cooled, slice thinly and serve with **Italian-Style Tuna Mayonnaise**, page 59, or **Parsley Parmesan Sauce**, page 100, as part of a luncheon or salad buffet.*

2 turkey tenderloins, about 10 to 11 oz. each
3 cups water

Spray a small plate with nonstick cooking spray. Plate should fit into rice cooker container with about ½-inch clearance for steam circulation. Place tenderloins in one layer on plate and cover with plastic wrap. Place plate on a small can with both ends cut out, or rack to support plate above water. Cover rice cooker and cook for about 25 minutes after water has come to a boil. Check at 20 minutes with an instant meat thermometer. Turkey should reach about 160°, and not be pink in the center. Remove from cooker and refrigerate if not serving immediately.

PARSLEY PARMESAN SAUCE

Makes 2/3 cup

This piquant green sauce is delicious on sliced cooked meats, plain pasta or rice. Make it at least an hour before serving so the flavors can combine. It keeps well refrigerated for several days, but bring to room temperature before serving.

leaves of 1 large bunch Italian parsley
 (about 2 cups leaves loosely packed)
2 garlic cloves
2 canned anchovies, drained
2 tbs. capers, drained

1/3 cup full-flavored olive oil
1 tsp. Dijon mustard
2 tbs. grated Parmesan cheese
1 tbs. lemon juice
salt and freshly ground pepper

Using the food processor, with the motor running, drop garlic in feed tube and process until chopped. Add washed, dried parsley leaves and process until well chopped. Add remaining ingredients and process until well combined but not smooth. Pour into a small bowl, cover and allow to stand 1 hour before using.

If using a blender, mince garlic and anchovies. Chop parsley by hand. Add olive oil, mustard and lemon juice to blender container and process until well mixed. Add chopped garlic, anchovies, parsley, capers, Parmesan cheese, salt and pepper to oil mixture and blend for a few seconds until well combined but not smooth.

STEAMED GARDEN VEGETABLES

Steamed vegetables retain vitamins and other nutrients that are sometimes poured down the drain when vegetables are boiled. If you are new to steaming vegetables, you will be delighted with the fresh taste and texture.

Artichokes particularly are great when steamed. You will also find steaming vegetables is quick and easy.

The traditional stainless steel or one of the new plastic collapsible steamer baskets make a useful insert for the rice cooker to hold vegetables during the steaming process. If you are using a small rice cooker (3-cup capacity), a mini-steamer basket will fit.

We generally do not salt vegetables before steaming, but add seasonings to the cooked vegetables.

In addition to the variety of vegetables that can be steamed, included are two delicious vegetable custards, *Savory Mushroom Timbales* and *Steamed Carrot and Orange Timbales*, that are steamed in the rice cooker. Steamed vegetables can be dressed up with a special sauce, or simply served with butter. Recipes are included for a piquant *Dijon Mustard Sauce*, a garlicky mayonnaise, *Aïoli*, as well as some easy vinaigrettes.

STEAMED ARTICHOKES

Steamed artichokes are a snap to do in the rice cooker. The size of your cooking container will limit the number of artichokes you can place in one layer and cook at the same time.

trimmed artichokes
2¾ cups water

Wash artichokes. Cut off artichoke stem and remove about 1 inch from top. Pull off 2 or 3 layers of outer leaves. Trim remaining uncut leaves straight across with scissors. Trim rough edges of artichoke bottom where leaves were removed.

Spray cooking container and steamer plate with nonstick spray. Add water and place artichokes leaf side down on steamer plate. Cover and cook for about 35 to 45 minutes, depending on size. Artichoke is done when bottom is easily pierced with a knife. If artichoke bottom is not tender, cover and let steam for a few more minutes. Remove to a serving platter.

Serve artichokes warm or at room temperature with *Easy Mayonnaise*, page 125, *Dijon Mustard Sauce*, page 127, or melted butter.

AROMATIC HERBED ARTICHOKES

Artichokes have an affinity for tarragon and other herbs. These make delicious picnic fare.

trimmed artichokes
2¾ cups water

FOR EACH ARTICHOKE, COMBINE:
1 tbs. olive oil
1 tsp. lemon juice
2 tbs. dry white wine
1 tbs. finely minced onion
1 tbs. finely chopped Italian parsley
¼ tsp. dried tarragon
salt and freshly ground pepper

Wash artichokes and cut off bottom stem. Cut about 1 inch from top of artichoke. Remove 2 or 3 layers of outer leaves; trim artichoke bottom. Pull out a few of the thorny center leaves to make a small cup for olive oil herb mixture, and gently flatten artichoke to spread leaves slightly apart.

Spray cooking container and steamer plate with nonstick spray and add water. Place artichokes stem down on steamer plate. Gently spoon olive oil herb mixture into spread leaves and center cup of artichoke. Cover cooker and steam for about 35 to 45 minutes, depending on size of artichoke.

Remove from container to serving plate. Pour in a small amount of water into container after artichokes are cooked for easy cleanup. Serve warm or cool with *Easy Mayonnaise*, page 125, or another sauce.

VARIATION

Substitute dried Greek oregano for the tarragon and Balsamic vinegar for the lemon juice. Makes a great side dish for grilled meats or serve with a deli platter and hot garlic bread.

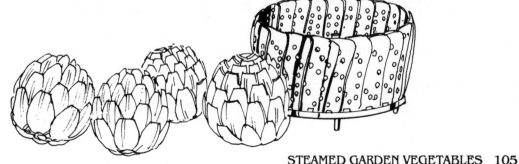

STEAMED NEW POTATOES

Small new potatoes (1 to 2 inches diameter) cook beautifully in one layer in the rice cooker. A collapsible steamer basket works well for this or use the steamer plate. Spray the cooking container and steamer plate, if using, with nonstick spray. Add scrubbed unpeeled potatoes in one layer with 1½ cups water. Cover and cook until potatoes are tender, about 20 minutes after the water starts to boil. Test potatoes: if not completely cooked, replace cover and allow to steam for another few minutes. If all the water has evaporated, pour a small amount of water into cooking container for easy cleanup. Serve hot with butter, salt and pepper; or with *Parsley Parmesan Sauce*, page 100; *Aïoli*, page 126; or use in one of the recipes which follow.

STEAMED NEW POTATOES WITH BUTTER AND PARSLEY

Melt 2 tbs. butter and combine with 1 tsp. lemon juice and 2 tbs. chopped parsley. Pour over hot potatoes in serving bowl, toss to combine, and serve.

NEW POTATO SALAD, page 61.
SMOKED SALMON AND NEW POTATO SALAD, page 58.

STEAMED SWEET POTATOES OR YAMS   Makes 1 cup

Steam sweet potatoes or yams in the rice cooker using a collapsible steamer basket. These are great served hot with a little butter, or puree them and make a **Steamed Sweet Potato or Yam Pudding***, page 133.*

1 lb. sweet potatoes or yams
1½ cups water

Peel and cut potatoes in 1-inch cubes and place in a steamer basket. Spray the rice cooker container with nonstick cooking spray, add 1½ cups water, cover and turn on. Bring water to a boil and carefully lower steamer basket into rice cooker. Cover and cook about 17 minutes. Test for doneness with a fork. Remove from rice cooker and serve immediately.

SWEET CORN

Sweet corn steams to perfection in the rice cooker. The size of the cooking container will limit the number of ears that can be cooked at one time.

fresh corn, trimmed   1 cup water

Remove corn husks and silk, and trim as needed. Spray rice cooker container and steamer plate with nonstick cooking spray. Place corn ears on steamer plate, add water, cover and cook about 10 minutes after water comes to a boil. Remove corn immediately.

BROCCOLI

Broccoli comes out of the rice cooker a pretty green color and you can cook it to the texture you like.

Spray rice cooker container and steamer plate with nonstick cooking spray. Cut broccoli into florets or pieces with 2 to 3 inch stems. Place on steamer plate or use a collapsible steamer basket and no steamer plate. Add 1 cup water. Cover and cook about 12 to 15 minutes after the water comes to a boil, to desired crispness. Remove broccoli to serving dish.

BROCCOLI ITALIAN-STYLE

Here is a delicious variation on plain steamed broccoli.

1 bunch broccoli, 1 to 1½ lbs.
3 tbs. full-flavored olive oil
1 garlic clove, minced
red pepper flakes
salt and freshly ground pepper
¾ cup water

Cut broccoli into florets or pieces with 2- to 3-inch stems. In a shallow plate, combine olive oil, garlic, red pepper flakes, salt and pepper. Add broccoli pieces and turn to coat with olive oil mixture. Spray rice cooker container and steamer plate with nonstick spray, or use a collapsible steamer basket and no steamer plate. Add broccoli pieces and ¾ cup water. Cover and steam about 15 minutes after water comes to a boil, or until broccoli is steamed to desired texture. Remove to serving dish and serve warm or at room temperature.

ASPARAGUS

Asparagus keeps its bright green color in the rice cooker. If you have time, peel the stems for more tender spears.

1 lb. asparagus, trimmed stems
½ cup water

Spray rice cooker container and steamer plate, if using one, with nonstick cooking spray. Arrange asparagus in a collapsible steamer basket or on steamer plate, and pour in water. Cook about 8 minutes after water comes to a boil, or until asparagus is cooked to desired tenderness. Remove asparagus spears immediately. If all water has evaporated, pour a little more water into cooking container for easy cleanup.

If you are serving the asparagus as a hot vegetable, dress with a little butter, salt and pepper, and serve immediately. For use in a salad, run cold water over cooked spears, place on paper towels, pat dry before adding your salad dressing.

MARINATED ASPARAGUS

Servings: 4

Cooked asparagus with a light orange, fresh ginger and soy sauce dressing makes a nice first course salad, or side dish. Marinate the asparagus while it is still a little warm to fully absorb the dressing flavors.

1 lb. cooked asparagus spears
1 tbs. olive oil
2 tsp. rice wine vinegar
1 tsp. sesame oil
1 tbs. soy sauce
¼ tsp. sugar
½ tsp. grated orange rind
½ tsp. grated fresh ginger
1 tbs. orange juice
salt and freshly ground pepper

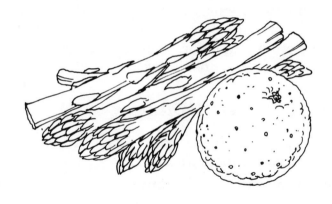

Dry cooked asparagus spears on paper towels, place in a shallow serving bowl. Combine remaining ingredients and pour over asparagus, turning spears until they are well coated with dressing. Serve at room temperature.

ASPARAGUS WITH ZESTY LEMON TOPPING

This is a quick fresh tasting topping for a pound of steamed asparagus.

2 tbs. unsalted butter
½ cup fresh bread crumbs

grated lemon rind from 1 lemon
1 tsp. lemon juice

Melt butter in a small skillet. When foaming, add bread crumbs and cook over medium heat until they start to brown. The crumbs turn brown very fast when they start changing color. Quickly add lemon rind and juice to crumbs and pour over cooked asparagus. Serve immediately.

SUGAR SNAP PEAS

Crisp sugar snap peas cook beautifully in the rice cooker. Use a collapsible steamer basket to hold them.

1 lb. sugar snap peas, stemmed

¾ cup water

Spray rice cooker container with nonstick cooking spray. Add water and steamer basket of sugar snap peas. Cover and cook about 8 to 10 minutes after water comes to a boil. Season and serve.

ORANGE GINGER CARROTS

Servings: 2 to 3

Carrots flavored with fresh ginger and orange are a colorful and delicious addition to any meal. If you like crisp tender carrots, remove them when they reach that degree of doneness. These can also be served at room temperature.

½ lb. carrots, peeled, sliced or cut into ½- x 3-inch strips
grated orange rind from 1 orange
½ cup orange juice or combination orange juice and water
2 slices fresh ginger root
1 tbs. butter

Spray rice cooker container with nonstick spray. Add carrots and remaining ingredients. Cover and cook for 10 to 12 minutes. Check to see if carrots are tender. If not, cover and continue to cook for 1 to 2 minutes more. Remove from pan and serve.

GREEN BEANS

Green beans have a nice texture when steamed in the rice cooker. A collapsible steamer basket is great for holding the beans. Good in a green bean salad.

1 lb. green beans, stemmed   1 cup water

Spray rice cooker container with nonstick spray. Place beans in a steamer basket. Cover and cook for 12 minutes after water comes to a boil. Check to see if beans are tender. If not, continue to steam 1 to 2 minutes longer. Carefully remove lid, place beans on platter, season and serve immediately, or allow to cool for use in another recipe.

ITALIAN ROMANO BEANS

Flat green Italian beans are delicious steamed and have a better texture than boiled.

1 lb. Romano beans, stemmed   1 cup water

Spray rice cooker container with nonstick cooking spray. Place beans in a steamer basket and lower into steamer. Cover and cook about 12 minutes after water comes to a boil. Check beans and continue to cook for another minute until they reach desired doneness. Season and serve immediately.

GREEN BEAN AND MUSHROOM SAUTÉ   Servings: 2 to 3

After you have steamed tender young green beans, add a few mushrooms and green onions to make a tasty side dish.

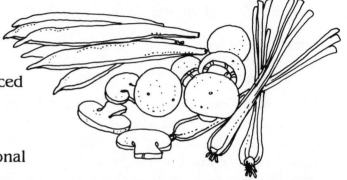

½ lb. cooked green beans
2 tbs. light olive oil
3 to 4 green onions, thinly sliced
5 to 6 medium mushrooms, thinly sliced
1 garlic clove, minced
2 tsp. cider vinegar
salt and freshly ground pepper
2 tbs. diced roasted red pepper, optional

Heat oil in a medium nonstick skillet and sauté onions and mushrooms over medium heat until mushrooms are soft. Add garlic and cook for another minute. Stir in cider vinegar; add salt, pepper, green beans and red pepper pieces, if desired. Cook, stirring, for 1 to 2 minutes to heat beans.

Serve immediately, or refrigerate and serve at room temperature on a lettuce leaf as a salad.

BRAISED LEEKS WITH MUSTARD VINAIGRETTE

Young small leeks about an inch in diameter are braised in vermouth and served with a mustard vinaigrette. Serve at room temperature on the buffet table or as a side dish for grilled meats.

4 to 6 small leeks, about 1- to 1½-
   inch diameter
1 cup water

1 cup dry vermouth
1 large garlic clove, smashed
2 sprigs parsley

Cut off all but about 1 inch of green leek top to make leek about 5 or 6 inches in length. Cut lengthwise down center to within an inch of root. Trim bottom of root, leaving it intact to hold leek together. Carefully spread leek leaves and wash under running water to remove sand. Spray rice cooker container with nonstick spray. Put in leeks and remaining ingredients, cover and cook about 18 to 20 minutes after water has come to a boil. Pierce leeks with a knife to see if they are tender. Remove from cooker and place in a shallow bowl. Pour *Easy Mustard Vinaigrette*, page 127, over, turning leeks to coat all sides. Allow to cool and serve at room temperature.

HERBED BRAISED CELERY

*Celery is delicious cooked in some chicken stock with dried herbs. Serve hot in a little of the cooking liquid, or marinate in **Easy Mustard Vinaigrette**, page 127.*

1 small bunch celery
3 cups chicken stock
1 tbs. dried onion flakes
½ tsp. dried thyme

¼ tsp. dried minced garlic
1 tbs. lemon juice
salt and freshly ground pepper

Remove 1 or 2 tough outer celery ribs, and cut off top of bunch so it is short enough to fit in rice cooker. Trim celery root end with a vegetable peeler but do not cut off. Save ribs and tops for the stock pot. Slice celery into quarters, lengthwise.

Spray rice cooker container with nonstick spray. Place celery quarters in cooker and add remaining ingredients. Cover and cook for about 35 to 40 minutes, until celery is tender. Turn cooker off and allow celery to cool in broth. If serving hot, place in serving bowl with a little of the cooking liquid. To serve cold, drain well and place in a shallow bowl. Pour *Easy Mustard Vinaigrette*, page 127, over celery, turning to coat all sides. Cover and chill in the refrigerator.

STEAMED BEETS

Vivid red beets are steamed in an orange-flavored liquid which is then reduced to make a quick sauce. Or make pickled beets after the beets are cooled and sliced. An all-purpose stainless steel or plastic steamer basket works well to hold the beets.

5 to 6 beets, about 2 inches in diameter
2½ cups water
rind and juice of 1 orange
1 tbs. rice wine vinegar
½ tsp. sugar
salt and freshly ground pepper

Cut off leafy beet tops to about 1 inch from beet. Wash, taking care not to break beet skin. Spray rice cooker and steamer basket with nonstick spray. Arrange beets in steamer; add water, orange rind and juice. Cover and cook for about 35 to 40 minutes, depending on size of beet. When beets are tender, remove beets to a plate and allow to cool. Peel beets, cut off tops and root ends, and slice.

Add rice wine vinegar, sugar, salt and pepper to rice cooker and continue to cook for about 8 to 10 minutes, reducing liquid to ⅓ cup. Taste for seasoning and add a little more vinegar if desired. Pour sauce over beets and serve warm.

PICKLED BEETS
After beets have been peeled and sliced, place in a glass or stainless steel bowl and add 3 to 4 red onion slices, if desired. Bring ¼ cup cider vinegar, ½ cup water and 2 tsp. sugar to a boil and pour over beets. Allow to cool. Cover and chill in the refrigerator for several hours.

SAVORY MUSHROOM TIMBALES

Vegetable custards make an easy, different vegetable preparation for those special dinners. They steam in about 20 minutes. Allow to stand for about 5 minutes, and then unmold. Four 6-oz. custard cups are a tight fit side by side in a medium size rice cooker, but you can place one on top, supporting it with the rims of the three lower cups. If you use smaller cups or timbales, steam for 15 to 18 minutes.

2 tbs. butter
½ lb. mushrooms, coarsely chopped
2 to 3 tbs. minced shallots or green
   onions
1 tbs. dried parsley
1 tsp. dried chives

⅓ cup heavy cream
1 tsp. Worcestershire sauce
¼ tsp. dried tarragon
2 eggs
salt and freshly ground pepper

Melt butter in a small skillet. Sauté mushrooms 3 to 4 minutes until they soften and release liquid. Add shallots, parsley and chives. Cook another 1 to 2 minutes to soften shallots. Allow to cool slightly. Pour mushrooms into container of a food processor with heavy cream and process until mixture is fairly smooth. Add Worcestershire, tarragon, eggs, salt and pepper. Pulse 7 to 8 times just to combine ingredients.

Spray custard cups or timbale molds with nonstick spray. Fill molds about ¾ full. Cover top of each mold with foil, crimping it near top of mold. Spray rice cooker container and steaming rack with nonstick spray. Add about 3 cups water to cooker. Place molds on steamer rack. Cover, turn cooker on and steam for 20 minutes after water comes to a boil. Turn cooker off and carefully remove timbales with kitchen tongs. Check one custard to make sure filling has set. Allow to stand for about 5 minutes. Remove foil. Run a thin knife blade around edge of timbales. Place a plate upside down on top of each timbale and invert. The timbale will unmold easily. Serve warm.

These reheat beautifully in the microwave, lightly covered with plastic wrap and cooked for 40 to 60 seconds on high.

STEAMED CARROT AND ORANGE TIMBALES

This pretty addition to any dinner plate goes together quickly if you have cooked carrots. Four 6-oz. custard cups are a tight fit side by side in a medium size rice cooker, but you can place one on top, supporting it with the rims of the three lower cups. If you use smaller cups or timbales, steam for 15 to 18 minutes.

2 tbs. butter
4 green onions, white part only, thinly sliced
2 cups cooked sliced carrots
orange rind from one orange
2 tbs. orange juice
2 tbs. heavy cream
2 eggs
salt and white pepper

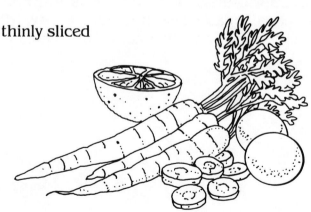

Melt butter in a small skillet. Sauté onions 1 to 2 minutes to soften. Combine onions, carrots, orange rind and juice, and cream in the bowl of a food processor. Process until mixture is quite smooth. Add eggs, salt and pepper and pulse 7 to 8 times just to combine ingredients. Spray 5- to 6-oz. custard cups or timbale molds with nonstick spray. Fill the molds about ¾ full and tightly cover each mold with foil. Crimp foil close to top of mold to avoid getting water into cup during the cooking process. Spray rice cooker container and steamer rack with nonstick spray and pour about 3 cups water into cooker. Place timbales on rack. Cover and steam for about 20 minutes after water has come to a boil. Remove molds from water with kitchen tongs. Check one custard to make sure filling has set. Allow to stand for about 5 minutes before uncovering and unmolding. Run a thin knife blade around edge of timbale to loosen and then place a plate upside down over mold and invert. The timbale will unmold easily. Serve warm. These reheat beautifully in the microwave, lightly covered with plastic wrap, 40 to 60 seconds on high power.

SUMMER SQUASH

Yellow or green squash are flavored with some chopped sweet basil and chives and steamed until tender. Use a collapsible steamer basket to hold the squash slices.

yellow squash or small green zucchini, cut into ¼- inch slices
1 tbs. olive oil
6 to 8 leaves fresh sweet basil, cut into slivers
1 tsp. minced chives or ½ tsp. dried
salt and freshly ground pepper
1½ cups water

Toss squash slices with oil, sweet basil, chives, salt and pepper and place in a steamer basket. Add water to rice cooker and turn it on. When water has come to a boil, lower steamer basket with squash into cooker, cover and steam for about 10 minutes until squash is the desired tenderness. Do not overcook.

EASY MAYONNAISE

Makes 1 cup

This is a quick recipe for the food processor or blender which can easily be doubled. This is perfect with artichokes and other steamed vegetables, fresh cooked crab or cold poached salmon.

1 whole egg at room temperature
1 tsp. lemon juice
1 tsp. white or rice wine vinegar
¼ tsp. salt
1 tsp. prepared Dijon mustard
generous dash of white pepper
¾ cup (approximately) canola or vegetable oil

Place all ingredients except oil in the food processor bowl fitted with a metal blade. Pulse a couple of times to combine. With the motor running, slowly add about a tablespoon of oil and allow to incorporate for a few seconds. Add remaining oil in a slow thin steam until mayonnaise reaches desired consistency.

AÏOLI

Makes 2¼ cups

This garlicky, full-flavored mayonnaise is the perfect accompaniment for almost any vegetable. Prepare a platter of the best fresh vegetables: steamed tiny new potatoes, tender sweet corn, thin or fat asparagus spears, artichokes, broccoli and cauliflowerets, little green beans. Add some crunchy carrot sticks, red pepper rings, tomatoes, and any other favorites; steamed shrimp or poached salmon if you want to be more elaborate; some bread sticks and you have great summer afternoon or evening party food.

6 to 8 garlic cloves, peeled
2 eggs at room temperature
juice of one lemon
1 tsp. salt
generous amount of white pepper

several drops of Tabasco
1 tsp. prepared Dijon mustard
¾ cup full-flavored olive oil
¾ cup vegetable oil

Drop garlic cloves through the feed tube of the food processor with motor running. Scrape down sides. Add remaining ingredients except 2 oils and process for a few seconds to combine. With motor running, slowly pour in a tablespoon or two of oil and allow to incorporate for a few seconds. Gradually add remaining oil in a slow thin stream until mixture forms a thick, shiny sauce. Refrigerate but allow to come almost to room temperature before serving.

DIJON MUSTARD SAUCE

Makes ½ cup

Here is a piquant mustard sauce that makes a great topping for steamed vegetables and also is a delicious dip for artichokes. Double recipe if you wish.

¼ cup prepared mayonnaise
2 tbs. Dijon mustard
2 tbs. milk

freshly ground pepper
½ tsp. sugar
¼ tsp. dried tarragon

Combine ingredients in a small bowl and stir until smooth and blended. Refrigerate if not serving immediately.

EASY MUSTARD VINAIGRETTE

Makes ¼ cup

*This zesty vinaigrette is great on **Braised Leeks**, page 116, **Herbed Braised Celery**, page 117 and any other vegetable to be served as an antipasto.*

¼ cup extra virgin olive oil
1 tbs. red wine vinegar

1 tsp. Dijon mustard
salt and freshly ground pepper

Whisk ingredients together in a small bowl until mixture forms an emulsion. Pour over cooked, drained vegetables. Allow vegetable to cool in vinaigrette or cover and refrigerate until ready to serve.

DESSERTS

For dessert, cook fresh summer fruits or steam puddings in the rice cooker. We have included recipes for a delicious *Strawberry and Rhubarb Bread Pudding*, a classic *Rice Pudding* and a *Chocolate Rice Pudding*, and a *Sweet Potato Pudding* with pumpkin pie spices. The rice cooker makes custards easily, and we offer two delicious examples.

STEAMED PEACHES

Fresh peaches are steamed with a little brown sugar and cinnamon for a simple delicious summer dessert.

2 large ripe peaches, peeled and seeded
2 tbs. brown sugar
½ tsp. cinnamon
1 cup water

Cut peaches into quarters. Place in a shallow dish that will fit inside rice cooker with ½-inch clearance around edges for steam to circulate. Sprinkle with brown sugar and cinnamon.

Pour 1 cup water into rice cooker container and place a platform or rack to support dish in bottom of container. Place dish with peaches on platform, cover rice cooker and steam about 5 to 7 minutes after water comes to a boil. Check at 5 minutes to see if peaches are tender. Remove dish from rice cooker and allow to cool. Serve at room temperature with a dollop of whipped cream or chill until ready to serve.

PEACHES WITH RASPBERRIES

Servings: 3 to 4

Fresh ripe peaches and raspberries are steamed together to make a picture-perfect dessert. Serve over vanilla ice cream or with a little whipped cream.

2 fresh ripe peaches, peeled, cut in half and seeded
12 to 15 fresh raspberries
1 tbs. sugar
2 tbs. Triple Sec or Framboise liqueur
1 cup water

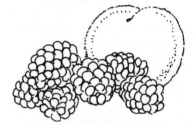

Place 4 peach halves cut-side up in a shallow bowl that will fit inside rice cooker container with ½-inch clearance. Sprinkle fresh raspberries over peaches and top with sugar and liqueur.

Pour 1 cup water in rice cooker container. Place a small platform or rack to hold bowl with peaches in bottom of rice cooker. Place peach bowl on top of platform. Cover rice cooker and cook about 10 minutes after water has come to a boil. Check at 8 minutes to see if peaches are tender. Do not overcook. Remove bowl of peaches from rice cooker and allow to cool before serving. Serve with whipped cream or over ice cream.

POACHED APPLES

Servings: 3 to 4

Use the rice cooker to make poached apples flavored with apple juice and cinnamon. Serve these for breakfast or as a light dessert with frozen yogurt.

3 cups apple juice
¼ cup sugar
1 tbs. lemon juice
1 slice of fresh ginger
1 cinnamon stick
3 to 4 cooking apples, or Golden Delicious, peeled, cored, cut into quarters

Spray the rice cooker container with nonstick spray. Add all ingredients except apples and turn rice cooker on. Cover and bring to a boil so sugar dissolves; continue to cook 3 to 4 minutes while you are preparing apples. Add peeled apples to liquid, cover and cook about 10 minutes or until apples are tender when pierced with a knife. Turn off rice cooker and carefully remove cover. Lift out cooker container and place on a rack to cool. Remove apples and liquid to a serving dish, place in refrigerator and chill until ready to serve.

WINE POACHED PEARS

Servings: 4

Any white wine or a Riesling makes a good poaching liquid for pears. The poaching liquid can be reduced and a little served with the chilled pears.

4 medium pears, firm but ripe
2 cups white wine
½ cup sugar
½ tsp. vanilla

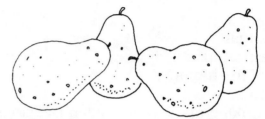

Peel pears and remove core from bottom. Cut a slice from bottom of pear to form a flat base. Leave stem on top of pear. Spray rice cooker container and steamer rack with nonstick spray. Add white wine and sugar to rice cooker container. Place pears on rack, cover and start rice cooker. Check pears at 20 minutes and continue to cook another 2 to 3 minutes if a knife blade does not easily pierce pear.

Remove pears from cooker to a plate. Continue to cook liquid uncovered for another 6 to 7 minutes to reduce. Add vanilla to liquid and pour over pears. Chill 1 to 2 hours or overnight in the refrigerator.

STEAMED SWEET POTATO
OR YAM PUDDINGS

Wonderful pumpkin pie flavors. Serve with a dollop of sweetened whipped cream.

1¼ cups cooked, pureed sweet
  potato or yam (about 1 lb. raw)
⅓ cup sugar
½ cup half and half or light cream
2 eggs

½ tsp. cinnamon
¼ tsp. nutmeg
¼ tsp. powdered ginger
pinch of powdered cloves
pinch of salt

Puree cooked sweet potato or yam in the food processor. Add remaining ingredients and process until smooth. Spray four 4- to 6-oz. custard cups with nonstick cooking spray. Fill about ¾ full with pudding mixture. Cover each cup with a foil cap, crimping foil close to top of cup. Place 2 cups water in rice cooker container with a steamer plate. Arrange custard cups on plate, cover and cook for 20 minutes after water has come to a boil. If using smaller cups, cook for 15 to 18 minutes after water has come to a boil. Remove cups from cooker with kitchen tongs and allow to stand for 5 minutes before uncovering. These are best served at room temperature or slightly chilled.

STEAMED RICE PUDDING

Creamy rice pudding is always a welcome dessert. Serve warm or chilled, with a strawberry sauce or sliced fruit. If you are using cold leftover cooked rice, add an extra 1/4 cup milk to the recipe below.

COOKED RICE
1 cup short grain Arborio or Silver Pearl rice
2 cups water

Spray rice cooker container with nonstick cooking spray. Add rice and water and cook until rice cooker shuts off. Allow to steam 10 minutes before using.

1 cup cooked short-grain rice
3/4 cup milk
3 tbs. sugar
1 tsp. vanilla

1/8 tsp. lemon extra
pinch of salt
several grates of nutmeg
1 egg, lightly beaten

Combine cooked rice with milk in a small saucepan. Cook over medium heat until rice has mostly absorbed milk and mixture is creamy, about 10 minutes. Remove from heat; stir in sugar, vanilla, lemon extract, salt and nutmeg. Allow to cool for a few minutes before combining with egg. When rice mixture is lukewarm, beat in egg, mixing well. Spray four 6-oz. custard cups with nonstick cooking spray. Fill cups with rice mixture and cover each cup with a foil cap, crimping foil close to top of cup. Place 2 cups water in rice cooker container. Place custard cups on a steam rack in cooker, cover and cook 20 minutes after water has come to a boil. If using smaller cups, steam 15 to 18 minutes after water has come to a boil. Remove cups from cooker with kitchen tongs and allow to stand 5 minutes before uncovering. Serve warm, or at room temperature, or refrigerate.

CHOCOLATE RICE PUDDING

Servings: 4 to 6

Rice for use in puddings should be soft, so cook 1 cup of short grain rice with 2 cups of water in the rice cooker and allow to steam 10 minutes after the rice cooker shuts off. If you are using leftover rice that has not just been cooked, add another 1/4 cup milk to the following recipe.

1 cup cooked short grain rice, Silver Pearl or Arborio
3/4 cup milk
dash of salt
2 oz. chocolate (Hershey's Special Dark), melted
1/4 cup sugar
1 tbs. dark rum or brandy
1 tsp. vanilla
1/4 tsp. cinnamon
2 eggs

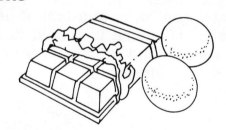

Place cooked rice and milk in a small saucepan. Cook rice over medium heat until most of the milk has been absorbed and mixture is creamy, about 10 minutes. Stir in salt, chocolate, sugar, rum, vanilla and cinnamon. Let rice mixture cool slightly before combining with eggs so eggs aren't cooked immediately upon contact with rice. Beat eggs until well combined. Carefully mix a spoonful of warm rice with eggs, and continue adding a little more rice until rice mixture has warmed beaten eggs, and then add remaining rice. Spray four 6-oz. custard cups with nonstick spray and fill about ¾ full. Cover each cup with foil, crimping foil near top of cup. Place a steamer rack in rice cooker and add 2 cups water. Place custard cups on steaming rack, cover and steam for 20 minutes after water has come to a boil. Remove cups from rice cooker with kitchen tongs and allow to cool for a few minutes before removing foil. Serve warm or refrigerate and serve chilled.

Note: If using smaller cups (4 to 5 oz.), steam for 15 to 18 minutes after water has come to a boil.

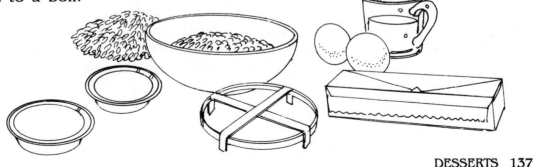

STEAMED RHUBARB AND STRAWBERRIES Servings: 4

*Strawberries and rhubarb are a classic combination. Steam them in the rice cooker and chill. Eat as a light dessert, or use in a **Strawberry Rhubarb Bread Pudding**, page 140.*

½ lb. rhubarb, trimmed and cut into 1-inch pieces
½ lb. strawberries, stemmed and quartered
½ cup sugar

Combine rhubarb, strawberries and sugar in a 7- to 8-inch stainless steel or glass deep dish for steaming. Pour 2 cups water into rice cooker container. Place a steamer plate or small rack in bottom of rice cooker container and place bowl with rhubarb and strawberries on rack. Turn rice cooker on, and after water has come to a boil, steam rhubarb for 10 to 12 minutes. Carefully remove the lid and check to see if rhubarb is soft; if not, steam for another 2 to 3 minutes. When rhubarb is soft, remove bowl from steamer and allow to cool.

STRAWBERRY SAUCE

This is a simple sauce that adds color and a fresh strawberry accent for steamed puddings or ice cream.

1 basket strawberries, stemmed, washed
¼ cup sugar
2 tbs. Triple Sec or Framboise liqueur

Combine all ingredients in a food processor or blender and process until smooth. Pour through a coarse sieve and use as a sauce for puddings or on ice cream.

VARIATION

Add 1 basket of fresh raspberries or boysenberries to the strawberries and increase the sugar to ½ cup. Process and strain.

STRAWBERRY RHUBARB BREAD PUDDING   Servings: 4

This old-fashioned dessert is easily done in the rice cooker and goes together quickly if you have already steamed the rhubarb and strawberries (see page 138). If you have some leftover brioche or other firm white bread, it is perfect for this dessert. Spoon some of the steamed rhubarb and strawberries around the pudding for a colorful sauce, or serve with **Strawberry Sauce***, page 139.*

2 eggs
¼ cup heavy cream
¼ tsp. cinnamon
generous grind of nutmeg
dash of salt and black pepper
1 cup steamed rhubarb and strawberries, very well drained
1 cup day old dry bread, crusts removed, cut or crumbled into ½-inch pieces

Spray four 6-oz. custard cups or ramekins with nonstick cooking spray. In a small bowl, beat eggs with a fork until well combined. Add remaining ingredients and beat until just mixed. If you have fresh strawberries, slice them and place 1 to 2 slices in the bottom of each custard cup. Fill cups about

¾ full with egg mixture. Cover each cup with foil. Pour 2 cups water in rice cooker container. Place a steamer rack in rice cooker and arrange filled dessert cups on top of rack. If the rice cooker is small, one cup can be wedged higher in cooker or supported with rims of three lower cups. When water has come to a boil, steam for 20 minutes. Remove cooked puddings from cooker and allow to cool. Run thin blade of a knife around edge of puddings and unmold. Spoon some steamed strawberries and rhubarb around puddings or serve with *Strawberry Sauce*, page 139.

COCONUT CUSTARD FLAN

This creamy custard is filled with flaked coconut and has a brown sugar sauce.

⅓ cup sugar
1 cup heavy cream
¼ cup sugar
dash salt

2 eggs plus 2 egg yolks
1 tsp. vanilla
⅛ tsp. almond extract
¼ cup dried flaked coconut

Place ⅓ cup sugar in a small nonstick skillet. Cook over medium heat until sugar melts and turns a deep shade of carmel. Warm a 3½-cup ovenproof dish (so the hot carmel will not crack it) that will fit into rice cooker. Pour hot carmel into dish, tilting so sugar mixture covers bottom of dish. Lightly beat together heavy cream, sugar, salt until sugar dissolves. Add remaining ingredients and mix well. Pour custard mixture on top of carmel. Add 3 to 4 cups water to rice cooker. Cover custard dish with foil and place on rack in cooker. Cover and cook for about 25 to 30 minutes after water comes to a boil. Check to see if mixture is firm. Carefully remove dish from rice cooker and allow to stand for a few minutes before unmolding, or chill in the refrigerator before serving.

LEMON CUSTARD

Serve this lemony dessert with fresh berries or strawberry sauce.

1 cup heavy cream
¼ cup sugar
dash salt
2 eggs

2 egg yolks
½ tsp. vanilla extract
½ tsp. lemon extract

Combine cream and sugar; beat until sugar dissolves. Add remaining ingredients and mix well. Spray four 6-oz. custard cups with nonstick cooking spray. Pour custard mixture through a sieve into custard cups. Cover each cup with a small piece of aluminum foil, crimping foil around top of cup. Add about 3 cups water to rice cooker container with a steaming rack in bottom of cooker. Place custard cups on rack. Cover and allow to steam about 20 minutes after water has come to a boil. Check on cup, recover and return to rice cooker for additional steaming if mixture is not firm to the touch. Remove from rice cooker and allow to stand for a few minutes before serving, or chill for a few hours.

Note: You can also pour mixture into a 3½-cup ovenproof dish that will fit into cooker. Cover with foil and steam 25 to 30 minutes after water comes to a boil.

OTHER THINGS YOU CAN DO IN A RICE COOKER

In addition to doing an excellent job in cooking rice and steaming vegetables, fish and chicken, the rice cooker can be used as an all purpose cooking pot for steaming sausages and hot dogs, boiling eggs, and cooking other grains such as millet, oatmeal, quinoa, barley and lentils.

The rice cooker makes a perfect steamer for dim sum, either those from a Chinese take-out or restaurant, or the ones included in this section. Use it for cooking frozen vegetables or entrées in a pouch, if you don't have a microwave*. The rice cooker's versatility comes into its own when you have limited cooking utensils.

*Heat cold rice by steaming in a bowl for a few minutes.

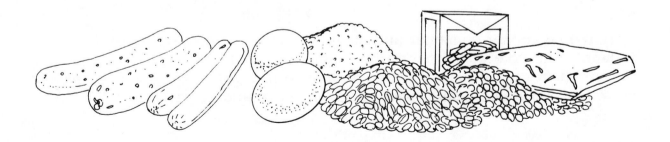

EGGS

Use your rice cooker for hard or soft boiled eggs. Be sure to make a small hole with a pin on the rounded end of each egg before cooking to keep it from cracking.

HARD-COOKED EGGS

eggs   1 cup water

Spray rice cooker container and steamer plate with nonstick cooking spray. Place eggs on steamer plate, add water, cover and cook 14 to 16 minutes after water boils. Remove eggs and place in bowl of cold water to cool.

SOFT BOILED EGGS

eggs   ½ cup water

Spray rice cooker container and steamer plate with nonstick cooking spray. Make a small hole with a pin on the rounded end of each egg before cooking to keep it from cracking. Place eggs on steamer plate, add water, cover and cook about 8 minutes after water boils. Remove and serve hot.

POACHED EGGS

Spray small custard cups or ramekins with nonstick cooking spray. Break one egg in each cup; season with salt and pepper, and add a sliver of butter if desired. Add 1 cup water to the rice cooker container, place steamer plate or rack in the bottom, and set the egg cups on the rack. Cover, bring water to a boil and cook until eggs reach desired firmness. Soft poached eggs generally cook in 5 to 6 minutes, and firmer eggs in 7 to 8 minutes.

Carefully remove egg cups from steamer, run the thin blade of a knife around the edge, and slide eggs onto individual warm serving plates, or on buttered toast. Serve immediately.

SMOKED SAUSAGES STEAMED IN BEER

Cooked sausages heat easily in the rice cooker. Spray cooking container and steamer plate with nonstick cooking spray. Place sausages on steamer plate, add ½ cup full-flavored beer or ale, cover and cook for 8 to 10 minutes.

Check to see if sausages are hot; if they are steaming, turn off cooker and remove to a serving platter. Serve with 2 to 3 different kinds of mustard, some potato salad, a crunchy vegetable tray and some more beer for a Monday night football party.

STEAMED GRAINS

Rice is only one of many interesting grains that can be cooked in the rice cooker. Barley and millet are nice alternatives to rice and can be used somewhat interchangeably with rice in stuffings and other preparations.

Quinoa, too, is a delicious variation that is easily cooked in the rice cooker. It is a nice foil for all the spices and herbs generally used with rice.

Millet looks and tastes a good deal like a more substantial couscous. Use it instead of rice in your chili bowl, with a curry sauce, or with a jar of your favorite spaghetti sauce. It also makes a great stuffing for peppers or tomatoes, or add eggs and make fritters. Buy hulled millet because the unhulled takes substantially longer to cook.

MILLET PARMESAN

The light fluffy millet grains can be compared to couscous in size and texture. Some good Parmesan cheese and a little butter folded into the cooked millet makes a terrific side dish that is similar to polenta and can be served with almost any entrée. When cooking millet, be sure to add either a little butter or oil so the grains remain separate when cooked.

½ cup uncooked hulled millet
1¾ cups chicken stock or water
1 tbs. butter

salt and freshly ground pepper
2 tbs. butter
½ cup Parmesan cheese

Toast millet grains in a heavy skillet over medium heat about 5 minutes until millet starts to lightly brown and smells lightly roasted. Spray rice cooker container with nonstick spray and add chicken stock, butter, salt and pepper. Add toasted millet to rice cooker; cover and cook about 40 minutes, until rice cooker turns off. Allow millet to steam for 10 minutes. Carefully remove the cover and stir in 2 tbs. butter and Parmesan cheese. Spoon into a warm serving bowl and serve immediately.

TOMATOES STUFFED WITH MILLET

Servings: 6

This is a colorful side dish to serve with grilled meats or as part of a light buffet. Millet makes a savory stuffing for almost any vegetable.

6 medium tomatoes
3 tbs. butter
1/4 cup diced onion
1 tsp. dried sweet basil or 3 tbs. fresh
2 tbs. fresh minced parsley, or 1 tsp. dried
1/2 tsp. salt
generous grinds of black pepper
1 1/2 cups cooked millet, page 149, without butter and cheese
1/4 cup grated Parmesan cheese

Cut a 1/2-inch slice off top of tomatoes. Carefully cut around center of each tomato with a small knife, leaving a 1/2-inch shell. Remove centers with a small sharp spoon and chop coarsely. Rinse out tomatoes to remove seeds and sprinkle inside of each tomato shell with a little salt. Turn shells upside down on a plate to drain for 15 to 20 minutes. Heat butter in a small skillet and sauté onions for 5 to 6 minutes until soft. Add sweet basil, parsley, salt, pepper, cooked millet and center tomato pieces. Cook for 1 to 2 minutes. Stir in 2 tbs. of Parmesan cheese. Fill tomatoes with millet mixture, dot with a little butter and sprinkle with remaining Parmesan cheese.

Place stuffed tomatoes on a small plate that will fit into rice cooker container; allow about ½-inch clearance for steam to rise. Place 1½ cups water in bottom of rice cooker container and place plate with tomatoes on a rack. After water has come to a boil, time tomatoes to steam for about 5 to 6 minutes, just until tomatoes are hot all the way through. Carefully remove tomatoes to serving plates. Serve hot or at room temperature.

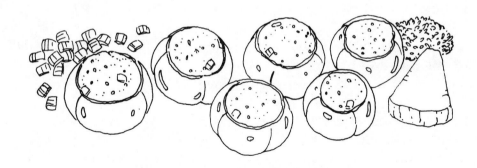

QUICK COOKED BARLEY

Servings: 4

Use the quick cooking pearled barley with some dried herbs and vegetables to make a hearty side dish, or use as a stuffing for peppers or tomatoes.

2 tbs. butter
2 tbs. dried onion pieces
2 tbs. dried parsley
1½ cups quick pearled barley
3¼ cups chicken stock
½ cup water
salt and freshly ground pepper

Spray rice cooker container with nonstick spray. Add all ingredients, cover and cook until rice cooker shuts off. Carefully remove cover and stir to loosen barley from bottom of pan. Re-cover and allow to steam for 5 minutes before serving.

GARDEN VEGETABLE BARLEY STEW

Servings: 4

Fresh vegetables cooked with barley make a hearty lunch or supper. Serve with some crisp garlic bread.

2 cups diced eggplant
3 cups chicken stock
1 cup quick pearled barley
2 tbs. butter
2 plum tomatoes, seeded and
  coarsely chopped
1 large red pepper, peeled and diced
2 small zucchini, cut in half lengthwise and sliced

1 large onion, cut in half and thinly
  sliced
2 cloves garlic, minced
1 tbs. dried or 3 tbs. fresh chopped
  parsley
1 tsp. dried thyme
½ tsp. dried or 2 tbs. chopped fresh
  sweet basil
salt and freshly ground pepper

Peel and dice eggplant and place it in a microwavable dish. Microwave on HIGH for 2 minutes, uncovered. Spray rice cooker container with nonstick spray. Add eggplant and remaining ingredients, cover, and cook for 20 minutes. Carefully remove cover, stir, and re-cover. Allow to steam for 10 minutes before serving. Pass grated Parmesan cheese, if desired.

BARLEY AND SUN-DRIED TOMATO PILAF

Servings: 4 as side dish

Barley makes an interesting substitute for rice in a pilaf, and the sun-dried tomatoes add a flavor punch.

2 tbs. full-flavored olive oil
½ cup chopped onion
1 cup pearled barley
2¼ cups chicken broth
1 tbs. dried or 2 tbs. fresh chopped
  parsley

¼ cup slivered sun-dried tomatoes,
  not oil packed
½ tsp. salt
freshly ground pepper
1 cup frozen green peas, defrosted

Spray rice cooker container with nonstick cooking spray. Add olive oil and turn rice cooker on. Sauté onion in oil for 2 to 3 minutes to soften; add barley and stir to coat with oil. Add remaining ingredients except for green peas. Cover and allow to cook until rice cooker shuts off. Carefully remove cover, quickly stir mixture and add green peas. Cover and allow to steam for 10 minutes before serving. Serve immediately.

COMPANY OATMEAL

This is a great treat for a cold winter morning or when you want a tasty breakfast for the children.

1⅓ cups Old Fashioned Quaker Oats
  (not quick cooking)
2 cups apple juice
¾ cup water
⅓ cup raisins
dash of salt

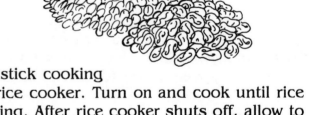

Spray rice cooker container with nonstick cooking spray. Add ingredients, stir and cover rice cooker. Turn on and cook until rice cooker turns off. Stir once during cooking. After rice cooker shuts off, allow to steam 10 minutes before serving.

QUINOA

Quinoa is a high-protein, natural, whole grain which cooks into a nutty, flavorful side dish. It can be used interchangeably with rice in many dishes, or cooked very simply with a few onion and parsley flakes.

1 cup quinoa	salt
2 cups water	1 tbs. dried onion flakes
1 tbs. butter or oil	1 tbs. parsley flakes

Spray rice cooker container with nonstick cooking spray. Add 1 cup rinsed or washed quinoa, water, butter or oil, salt, dried onion flakes and parsley flakes. Cover and cook until rice cooker shuts off. Carefully remove cover, stir and recover. Allow to steam for 10 minutes before serving.

VARIATIONS

Add 1 large chicken or beef bouillon cube to water. Use to stuff tomatoes or peppers, or as an accompaniment for *Easy Curry Sauce*, page 36, or with *Chicken Gumbo*, page 38.

CURRIED QUINOA PILAF

Servings: 4

The mild curry flavor makes this a delicious accompaniment for grilled meats or vegetables. Top with toasted slivered almonds and fresh cilantro leaves just before serving.

2 tbs. butter
1 tsp. curry powder
1/2 cup chopped onions
1 garlic clove, minced
1/3 cup coarsely grated carrot
1/4 cup freeze-dried mushroom pieces
　or 1/4 lb. fresh mushrooms, chopped
2 cups water

1 cup quinoa, rinsed with cold water,
　drained
salt and freshly ground pepper
1/2 tsp. lemon zest
1 tbs. lemon juice
1/4 cup white or dark raisins
1/4 cup slivered toasted almonds and
　fresh cilantro leaves for garnish

Spray rice cooker container with nonstick spray. Turn cooker on and melt butter. Add curry powder and cook 1 to 2 minuts to bring out curry flavor. Add onions, garlic, carrot and mushroom pieces. Cook, stirring, 1 to 2 minutes. Add water, quinoa, salt, pepper, lemon zest and juice. Cover rice cooker and cook until it shuts off. Carefully remove cover, stir in raisins, re-cover and allow to steam for 10 minutes. Spoon into a serving dish and top with almonds and cilantro. Serve immediately.

DIM SUM DELIGHTS

The rice cooker makes a great steamer to reheat the Chinese steamed buns and filled wrappers that you find in the market or Chinese take-out counters. Recipes follow for a Chinese-style steamed bun filled with a quick barbecue chicken filling, a great shrimp and pork *Shao Mai Dumpling*, steamed *Chicken Treasure Packages* in foil, and *Pearl Balls*.

BARBECUED CHICKEN BUNS

Makes 8

Flavor some cooked chicken with your favorite barbecue sauce and it makes a tasty filling for the Chinese-style steamed buns. The bun dough goes together quickly in the food processor.

1 cup all purpose flour
1 cup cake flour
2 tbs. sugar
2½ tsp. baking powder
1 tbs. vegetable shortening

⅔ cup milk
¾ cup cooked chicken, cut into
⅜-inch cubes
⅓ cup barbecue sauce

Add flours, sugar and baking powder to the food processor bowl. Pulse to mix well. Add shortening and pulse several times to combine. With processor running, add milk and process until dough forms a ball. Turn out dough onto a lightly floured board and knead for 1 to 2 minutes. Dough will be quite soft. Form dough into a log about 12 inches long. Cover with plastic wrap and allow to rest while preparing filling. Combine chicken pieces and barbecue sauce in a small saucepan. Heat through over low heat, stirring frequently so sauce doesn't stick or burn. Remove from heat and allow to cool before filling buns.

To form buns, cut dough into 8 equal pieces. Take a piece of dough and flatten into a 3- to 4-inch circle, thicker in the middle than on the edges. Put about 2 tbs. of filling in the middle of the circle and pull up sides of dough. Pleat and pinch dough to seal top. Place each bun on a 2-inch square of aluminum foil.

Place a small platform (a small 8-oz. can with both ends cut out or an artichoke holder) in rice cooker container to hold steamer plate about 2 inches above water. Add about 3 cups water to rice cooker container, cover and bring water to a boil. Place 4 buns on steamer plate and using a plate holder carefully place plate on small platform in rice cooker. Cover and steam for 10 minutes. Remove cooked buns with kitchen tongs and repeat steaming process with remaining 4 buns. These buns freeze well. Serve at room temperature or reheat by steaming over hot water for a few minutes.

SHAO MAI DUMPLINGS

Makes 15

*A Cantonese dim sum is not complete without these tasty steamed dumplings.
Use the round 3-inch wrappers, or cut square won ton wrappers into 3-inch circles.*

FILLING

1 dried black Shiitake mushroom
¼ lb. peeled, deveined small
  uncooked shrimp
¼ lb. lean ground pork
4 canned water chestnuts, finely
  diced

2 green onions, finely minced
1 tsp. fresh grated ginger
1 garlic clove, minced
1 tbs. oyster sauce or Worcestershire
  sauce
salt and white pepper

FOR ASSEMBLY

3-inch round shao mai wrappers

fresh cilantro leaves

DIPPING SAUCE

hot pepper oil
rice wine vinegar

soy sauce

    Cover dried mushroom with boiling water and let stand 15 minutes to soften.
Squeeze dry, cut out tough stem and chop finely. If preparing by hand, all in-

gredients including the shrimp should be finely chopped and then combined. If using the food processor, mince water chestnuts, onions, ginger and garlic in the food processor and then add remaining ingredients, pulsing a few times to chop finely. Do not over-process.

To assemble: Place about 1 tablespoon of the mixture in center of wrapper. Bring sides of wrapper up around filling, pleating wrapper a little to form a cup. The finished shao mai will look like a tiny cupcake showing the meat filling in the center. Place a fresh cilantro leaf over meat. Keep unused wrappers covered with a damp paper towel so they don't dry out.

To steam: Place about 2 cups of water in rice cooker container. Place a small platform or artichoke holder to hold the steamer plate in rice cooker container. Spray steamer plate with nonstick spray and arrange shao mai on plate about 1 inch apart. When water is steaming in rice cooker, carefully lower plate into rice cooker onto platform. Cover and steam for 15 minutes. Remove shao mai and serve immediately.

To serve: Pour a small amount of rice vinegar, soy sauce, and a few drops of hot pepper oil into small dishes. Dip shao mai into sauce. The cooked shao mai can be refrigerated and reheated in the microwave or steamed for a few minutes. These can also be assembled ahead, covered with plastic wrap and refrigerated before steaming. The recipe amounts can easily be doubled.

PEARL BALLS

Makes 18

*Remember to soak the rice about 2 hours before you start making these. Serve them with the same dipping sauce as for **Shao Mai**, page 160. Leftovers can be refrigerated and resteamed or reheated in the microwave the next day.*

½ cup Calrose rice, rinsed
¼ lb. uncooked shrimp, peeled, deveined
6 water chestnuts, diced finely
½ lb. lean ground pork
1 tbs. minced green onion, white part only
1 tsp. minced fresh ginger
2 tsp. soy sauce
½ tsp. sesame oil
½ tsp. sugar
salt and white pepper
1½ tbs. cornstarch
2 tsp. dry sherry

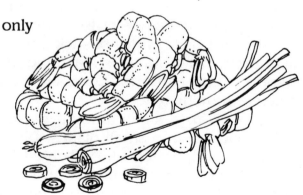

CHICKEN TREASURE PACKAGES

Makes 16 pieces

Tender pieces of chicken breast are marinated, and then wrapped in foil and steamed. These succulent morsels can be made ahead, refrigerated and steamed just before serving. The recipe can be increased to meet the demand.

2 boneless, skinless chicken breasts

MARINADE

½ tsp. fresh grated ginger
1 tbs. hoisin sauce
1 tbs. soy sauce
1 tbs. dry sherry or Shao xing rice
   wine

1 tsp. sesame oil
1 tsp. cornstarch

FOR ASSEMBLY

4 green onions, white part only,
   slivered
fresh cilantro leaves

16 pieces of foil, about 5 inches
   square

Cut chicken breasts into 8 pieces each. Combine marinade ingredients in a small bowl and add chicken pieces. Allow to stand for 15 minutes.

To assemble: Place a drained piece of chicken just below center of foil square. Top with slivers of green onions and 2 to 3 fresh cilantro leaves. Bring top half of foil piece down over chicken even with bottom edge of foil. Fold up about ¼-inch from bottom and then make a fold ¼-inch in from each side. Continue to fold up bottom and side edges until you can feel you are close to chicken piece inside foil.

Place a cup of water in rice cooker container. Bring to a boil, place foil packets on a collapsible steamer basket or rack, allowing room for steam to circulate around the packages, and lower into rice cooker. Cover and cook for 7 minutes. Remove packets from steamer and serve as an appetizer.

MARINATED MUSHROOMS

These piquant mushrooms keep well in the refrigerator for a few days and are a delicious addition to an antipasto or salad plate.

½ lb. button mushrooms
2 tbs. full-flavored olive oil
1 tbs. lemon juice
¼ cup rice wine vinegar
¼ cup dry sherry or white wine
1 garlic clove

¼ tsp. sugar
½ tsp. dried thyme
½ tsp. dried sweet basil
generous dash of red pepper flakes
salt and freshly ground pepper

Clean mushrooms and cut stems even with mushroom top. If mushrooms are large, cut into quarters. Spray rice cooker container with nonstick spray. Add all ingredients except mushrooms. Cover and bring to a boil, about 3 to 4 minutes. Add mushrooms and cook for 5 minutes. Turn off cooker and let mushrooms cool in liquid. Add salt and pepper to taste.

INDEX

SERVE CREATIVE, EASY, NUTRITIOUS MEALS WITH NITTY GRITTY® COOKBOOKS

The Versatile Rice Cooker
The Dehydrator Cookbook
Waffles
The Coffee Book
The Bread Machine Cookbook
The Bread Machine Cookbook II
The Bread Machine Cookbook III
The Bread Machine Cookbook IV
The Sandwich Maker Cookbook
The Juicer Book
The Juicer Book II
Bread Baking (traditional),
 revised
The Kid's Cookbook, revised
The Kid's Microwave Cookbook
15-Minute Meals for 1 or 2
Recipes for the 9x13 Pan

Chocolate Cherry Tortes and
 Other Lowfat Delights
Lowfat American Favorites
Lowfat International Cuisine
The Hunk Cookbook
Now That's Italian!
Fabulous Fiber Cookery
Low Salt, Low Sugar, Low Fat
 Desserts
What's for Breakfast?
Healthy Cooking on the Run
Healthy Snacks for Kids
Creative Soups & Salads
Quick & Easy Pasta Recipes,
 revised
Muffins, Nut Breads and More
The Barbecue Book

The Wok
New Ways with Your Wok
Quiche & Soufflé Cookbook
Cooking for 1 or 2
Meals in Minutes
New Ways to Enjoy Chicken
Favorite Seafood Recipes
No Salt, No Sugar, No Fat
 Cookbook
New International Fondue
 Cookbook
Extra-Special Crockery Pot
 Recipes
Favorite Cookie Recipes
Authentic Mexican Cooking
Fisherman's Wharf Cookbook
The Creative Lunch Box

Write or call for our free catalog.
Bristol Publishing Enterprises, Inc.
P.O. Box 1737, San Leandro, CA 94577
(800)346-4889; in California (510)895-4461